DAYBOOK 1918

Early Fragments

DAYBOOK 1918

Early Fragments

J. V. FOIX

Edited and translated by Lawrence Venuti

NORTHWESTERN UNIVERSITY PRESS

EVANSTON, ILLINOIS

Northwestern University Press
www.nupress.northwestern.edu

Support for this publication came in part through the Global Humanities Initiative,
which is jointly supported by Northwestern University's Buffett Institute for Global
Studies and the Kaplan Institute for the Humanities.

10 9 8 7 6 5 4 3 2 1

Library of Congress Cataloging-in-Publication Data

Names: Foix, J. V., author. | Venuti, Lawrence, editor, translator, writer of added
    commentary. | Foix, J. V. Diari 1918. Catalan. Selections.
Title: Daybook 1918 : early fragments / J. V. Foix ; edited and translated by Lawrence
    Venuti.
Description: Evanston, Illinois : Northwestern University Press, 2019. | Poems in the
    original Catalan and in English translation. | Includes bibliographical references.
Identifiers: LCCN 2019013951 | ISBN 9780810140653 (trade paper : alk.
    paper) | ISBN 9780810140660 (ebook)
Classification: LCC PC3941.F57 D513 2019 | DDC 849.9154—dc23
LC record available at https://lccn.loc.gov/2019013951

For K V D

It is so easy now to see gravity at work in your face
Easy to understand time, that dark process
To accept it as a beautiful process, your face

(Peter Gizzi)

Contents

Omitted Texts

Essays

Acknowledgments

While this project was under way, it went through more changes than typical translations, whether the result of bumps in the road or serendipitous breakthroughs, so that I have accumulated not only more but different debts than usual. First and foremost I must express my gratitude to Mar Rosàs Tosas, who is currently research coordinator in applied ethics at the Universitat Ramon Llull in Barcelona. She scrupulously examined the translations against Foix's Catalan texts, calling my attention to interpretive possibilities I might not have otherwise perceived and sharing with me her knowledge of Catalan, at once native and scholarly. I also benefited from the linguistic and literary expertise of Dolors Juanola Terradellas, formerly on the faculty of the Institut Jaume Salvador i Pedrol in Barcelona, whose comments are always sharp, learned, and witty. Joan Ramon Veny-Mesquida, professor of Catalan Philology at the Universitat de Lleida, allowed me to draw on his deep immersion in Foix's work by patiently answering my probing questions. The Oficina de Turisme of El Porta de la Selva, the Grup Mineralògic Català, and Salvador Palomar, the blogger at "La Teiera," all supplied useful information. None of my Catalan informants can be held responsible, of course, for whatever use I made of their help.

I received much-needed encouragement from a number of colleagues and friends, particularly Maria Dasca Batalla, Francesc Parcerisas, Joan Ramon Resina, and Mario Santana. Sònia Garcia of the Institut Ramon Llull graciously helped me secure a copy of Veny-Mesquida's monumental edition of the *Diari 1918*. I would like to thank Andrew Peart, Rachael Allen, and Daniel Simon, editors at *Chicago Review*, *Granta*, and *World Literature Today*, respectively, for hosting some of the translations in their magazines. Sophie Collins generously included a group of texts in her anthology, *Currently & Emotion: Translations* (London: Test Centre,

2016). Margarida Trias, director of the Fundació J. V. Foix, and Jordi Madern Mas, president, gave their support from the very beginning. I owe a special debt to Senyora Trias for providing a range of pertinent materials.

All unattributed translations in the introduction and notes are mine. They have been prepared in accordance with the interpretive occasions that they are intended to serve.

The verse in the dedication is excerpted from Peter Gizzi's poem "Lines Depicting Simple Happiness," which appears in his collection *The Outernationale* (Middletown, Conn.: Wesleyan University Press, 2007). It is used with the kind permission of the poet.

L.V.
New York–Barcelona–Syros
June 2018

Introduction

The poet Josep Vicenç Foix i Mas (1893–1987) is a major figure in modern Catalan literature who has influenced generations of writers down to the present. Under the pen name of J. V. Foix (his surname is pronounced "Fosh" with a long "o"), he published many individual volumes, but his greatest achievements consist of three books. *Sol, i de dol* (Alone, and In Mourning, 1947), a collection of seventy sonnets that address such themes as love and the role of the poet, synthesizes Foix's traditional and avant-garde interests by drawing on medieval poetry in Catalan, Provençal, and Italian, including the work of Ausiàs March, Bernart de Ventadorn, and Guido Cavalcanti. *Les irreals omegues* (The Unreal Omegas, 1949), a poem in thirteen sections, develops a symbolist style to address the problems of living during the Spanish Civil War and after, under Franco's fascist regime, which enforced strict censorship and sought to suppress the Catalan language. In the *Diari 1918* (*Daybook 1918*), a collection of prose poems, Foix's writing turns oneiric as he endows recognizably Catalan customs and geography with a surrealist quality.

Between roughly 1909 and 1925, Foix got into the habit of making diaristic notes that recorded experiences, reflections, ideas, and images. These notes became the basis of two kinds of prose texts—one autobiographical, chronicling his encounters with mentors and associates, the other poetic, exploring a lyric vein in fragmentary narratives. It is these poetic narratives that came to form the *Diari 1918*. Foix initially planned the project as a collection of three hundred sixty-five prose poems, one for each day of the year, but he completed only 203, which he published in book-length selections over several decades before gathering them into one volume in 1981. He put the texts from the start of his career in a section he called "primers fragments" ("early fragments"), work that began appearing in 1918 in periodicals and then in his first two books, *Gertrudis* (1927) and

KRTU (1932). These early fragments constitute the core of the translation that follows.

✳ ✳ ✳

At the beginning of the twentieth century, a number of Catalan writers and artists looked to the modernist avant-garde movements in Europe to invigorate native literary and artistic traditions. They were gauging the aesthetic and political value of diverse experimental practices as Catalonia itself experimented with autonomous government before the advent of Franco's dictatorship in 1939. Foix in particular saw himself as an "investigator in poetry," exploring a variety of poetics, and he conducted his investigations not only in poems but also in the many notes, articles, and essays he published in the periodicals which were then proliferating in Catalonia, especially in Barcelona. These newspapers and magazines were filled with nationalist pronouncements and debates even as the contributors busily welcomed foreign literature and art through imitations and translations as well as commentary.

For the biweekly *La Revista* Foix wrote a column that surveyed the contents of periodicals in various countries, including Argentina, France, Italy, and Spain. In 1918, for instance, he presented the latest issue of Pierre Reverdy's journal, *Nord-Sud*, summarizing Reverdy's account of the poetic image. In the same year, Foix assumed the editorship of *Trossos* (Pieces), a magazine that became an important vehicle for his work even though it lasted only six issues. As editor he ran brief accounts of Cubism and Futurism and announced the Parisian publication of Guillaume Apollinaire's play *Les mamelles de Tirésias* (The Breasts of Tiresias, 1918), where the French writer coined the term "surrealist." In the same magazine, Foix also published his Catalan translations of poems by Philippe Soupault and Ezio Bolongaro, as well as two of his own surrealist narratives. This activity points to the significance of the year 1918 for him: it represents a watershed in his development as a writer.

Foix's most important contribution to the Catalan press proved to be his work for *La Publicitat*, a daily newspaper that became the organ of the nationalist political party, Acció Catalana. Between 1922 and 1936, when the Spanish Civil War erupted, Foix published several hundred articles in variously titled columns ("Meridians," "Itineraris," "Panorama Universal de les Lletres," among others), anonymously at first, then under his name or initials, and finally with a succession of pseudonyms. He commented on decisive political events at home and abroad, criticizing the rise of fascism in Germany and in Italy and the repressiveness of the Soviet Union under Stalin. Although he admired the nationalist dedication of Charles Maurras's Action Française, he rejected the French ideologue's monarchism. "For us," Foix wrote in 1931, "Catalanism has always been an essentially republican movement." He discussed canonical works of Catalan literature, such as Ramon Llull's *Llibre de les Bèsties* (c. 1287) and Joanot Martorell and Martí Joan de Galba's chivalric romance, *Tirant lo Blanc* (1490). He emphasized contemporary thinkers, writers, and artists to whom he was especially attracted, discussing the work of Henri Bergson and Sigmund Freud, Alexander Blok and André Breton, Giorgio de Chirico and Max Ernst. Between 1930 and 1936, *La Publicitat* also ran Foix's Catalan versions of Paul Éluard's poetry.

These interventions were designed to increase the sophistication of Foix's readers. He militated against any provinciality by examining Catalan cultural and political issues in relation to the latest international developments. In effect, he was instructing Catalans on how to read his own cosmopolitan poetry by documenting his various affiliations, foreign as well as domestic.

Still, Foix did not assign equal value to every Catalan reception of foreign currents, particularly where the modernist avant-gardes were concerned. In "Avant-gardism," a 1921 essay for the monthly *Monitor: Gaseta Nacional de Política, d'Art i de Literatura*, he likened the "patriotic upstartism" that appears in "every nationalism" to the "fever to draw attention to themselves" that infected "some avant-gardists." He particularly lamented Catalan experiments "that, lacking control and tending directly toward the mutilation of the language at the moment of its rehabilitation, could exert a dangerous influence." In mentioning the "rehabilitation" of Catalan, he was referring to the efforts of the linguist Pompeu Fabra to standardize the orthography and grammar of the language, culminating in the publication of Fabra's *Diccionari General de la Llengua Catalana* (1932). Foix acknowledged his own commitment to literary innovation, but he regarded "avant-gardism" as potentially "one of the factors that disrupt the stylistic elevation of our language." The challenge he saw facing the Catalan writer was how to prevent cosmopolitanism from devolving into "a confusion of diverse tendencies and clumsy applications" that would undermine a nationalist investment in Catalan literature.

Foix's interest in modernist experimentalism situated him in the margins of the contemporary cultural scene in Catalonia, where groups of writers and artists who reflected broader European trends vied for dominance. *Modernisme*, which despite its name was not an avant-garde but a decadent movement comparable to Art Nouveau, produced stunning achievements in architecture, painting, and the decorative arts, the work of turn-of-the-century figures like Antoni Gaudí and Ramon Casas. It also gave rise to a vibrant narrative and dramatic literature that questioned middle-class values and explored social problems. The most esteemed poet was Joan Maragall (1860–1911), who advocated a poetics of Nietzschean vitalism in his notion of the "paraula viva" ("living word"), a spontaneous use of language. Maragall's 1904 poem "L'ametller" (The Almond Tree) exemplifies his romantic approach, translated here so as to evoke comparable nineteenth-century British poetries:

> Midmost on the side of the mountain
> I spied a blossoming almond tree:
> White flag, God grant you protection—
> ah the days when you delighted me!
> You are the peace that you announce
> betwixt the sun and cloud and wind . . .
> The best climate has not yet beckoned,
> but you bear its utter jubilance.

In a notebook entry from 1911, Foix called Maragall's bluff, casting doubt on the authenticity of this poetry:

> Wherever spontaneity, holy spontaneity, may exist—I would like to see the original drafts of the naïve adherents of spontaneity—there's a hitch. The spontaneity of the word in every farmhouse, in every individual—which are Maragall's preferred discourses—is typically the strident cry and the crude expression.

Maragall's verse, in contrast, is characterized by linguistic and prosodic refinement. Foix shrewdly saw that these features belie Maragall's vitalist claim that the poet enjoys a privileged connection to nature.

Foix entered into a more complicated relationship with *Noucentisme*. This somewhat later movement reacted against the romantic excesses typified by Maragall and, although modern in orientation, prized a poetic classicism that cultivated ornate styles. Coined by the writer Eugeni d'Ors (1881–1954), the term plays on the Catalan word for both "nine" and "new" ("nou") to refer to the twentieth century, the 1900s ("milnoucent" in Catalan), following Italian labels for historical periods like "cinquecento" (the 1500s or the sixteenth century). The daily newspaper with the widest circulation, *La Veu de Catalunya* (The Voice of Catalonia), became an important venue for *Noucentisme*, which found its most articulate spokesman in d'Ors. From 1906 to 1920 he contributed a column called *Glosari* (Glossary), where he spun urbanely ironic anecdotes that served to illustrate the principles of the movement.

On 23 June 1910, for example, the newspaper ran the column with a piece titled "Coets" (Rockets). The date marks the eve of the Feast of Sant Joan, or Saint John the Baptist, which Catalans celebrate with such rituals as bonfires and fireworks. Not only did d'Ors couch his parable in a custom that would be immediately familiar to his readers, he ingeniously exploited the appearance of Halley's Comet in April of that year:

> A warm night in June. A Barcelonan steps out onto his terrace, fires off a rocket, and harks back to Halley's Comet.
>
> As when the comet had passed, some time ago, every danger has now ceased, and the Barcelonan amuses himself with some philosophizing, some imagery.
>
> He thinks: the comet is to the rocket as a tiger is to a cat.
>
> A rocket is a domesticated comet.
>
> It is a paradox, furthermore, that the charm of comets in a wild state—stars with a tail—consists in calculated appearances, while the charm of comets in a domestic state—that is to say, rockets—consists in being unforeseen.
>
> This point disagrees with any suspicion that civility is something with a fixed geometry.
>
> On the contrary: Wildness is always a hugely fixed thing, since it leaves much room for the fated. Civility is a divine flower of contingency.
>
> Rise, rise to the heights, unforeseen rockets, contingent rockets—norms!—freedoms!

For d'Ors, the rocket functions as an eloquent symbol that expresses the *Noucentista* advocacy of innovation ("freedoms") through constraint ("norms").

Foix's attitude toward this sort of writing was ambivalent at best. In another notebook entry from 1911, he disparaged the *Noucentista* author's style as displaying the "preciosity and decadence of the fin de siècle," producing "a Pre-Raphaelite, Ruskinian, even Wildean flavor which does not fade despite the strong classicizing compulsion of the commentator, so lucid, intelligent, astute, and incisive." Foix clearly shared Ezra Pound's critical view of nineteenth-century poeticism, what Pound called "the crust of dead English" that had "obfuscated" him in his poems and translations. Not only did Foix articulate a modernist criticism of British Romantic and Victorian poetry and use it to assess Catalan literary developments, he seems to have been thinking along these lines before Pound published his own remarks in essays like "A Retrospect" (1918) and "Guido's Relations" (1929).

The uncanniness of this coincidence does not stop here. Foix's knowledge of English was limited. Whatever he knew of anglophone writing was derived mostly, if not entirely, from translations—Catalan, Castilian, French. He published his Catalan versions of excerpts from T. S. Eliot's *The Waste Land* (1922) soon after the poem appeared, although these versions were made from a French translation. Foix's critique of d'Ors's prose testifies to the international reach of modernism as well as to his intuitive comprehension of its ideas.

* * *

Noucentisme was deeply invested in Catalan nationalism, and that investment, particularly as articulated by Eugeni d'Ors, can be distinguished from Foix's ideological standpoint. The difference becomes evident in d'Ors's 1909 piece "Metics," where in reviving this ancient Greek term for foreign residents he followed contemporary French nationalists like Charles Maurras. In an 1894 article published in the right-wing newspaper *La Cocarde*, Maurras had denounced groups that he viewed as divisive and therefore threatening to the French nation, namely, Protestants, Masons, Jews, and "Métèques." While setting aside Maurras's Catholicism and anti-Semitism, d'Ors did share his xenophobia: "Metics" stigmatizes working-class immigrants, specifically citing "concierges and tram conductors" as weakening the emergent national community because they resist the "demographic expansion" of the Catalan language. D'Ors's vernacular nationalism goes hand in hand with a cultural "imperialism," as he himself called it. He demands the assimilation of foreigners to the "literary and intellectual" values of an indigenous, Barcelona-based elite who, unlike their Parisian counterparts, lack the cosmopolitanism that might enable them to withstand the "infiltration" of cultural differences.

Foix's modernism led him to conceive of a Catalan national culture that was much more open. In a 1933 article for *La Publicitat*, he addressed the question "Is there a Catalan school of superrealism?" while taking Salvador Dalí's paintings as his case. "We do not believe in a Catalan racial type," wrote Foix, "or in nationalism of a racial type," but he found that Dalí exemplifies a curious "paradox": he is a painter who is "ideologically without a homeland," even "a denier of the homeland," although he made his contribution to "universal painting" because of "his fidelity to the spirit of the tribe that gave birth to him." Dalí is a "European" surrealist precisely because his brand of "realism" is "profoundly, exclusively local"—that is to say, Catalonian, by which Foix seemed to refer to the striking landscapes in Dalí's paintings. In the 1935 essay "Homeland," Foix makes clear his opposition to any form of nationalism that is so assimilated to dominant ideologies at home as to subvert transnational values, including those that he felt should be seen as universal.

Nonetheless, Foix struggled to define the relation between his writing and the Catalan political situation. In his 1929 essay "Some Reflections on One's Own Literature," he expresses his belief that "some" of his writing occupies an ideological "position" that is "loyal" to Catalanism. To articulate this position, he describes two important decisions he made in his fledgling career: on the one hand, he discloses his "youthful ambition" to withhold his signature from what he describes as "the literary objectivation of [his] psychic states," the body of writing that would become the *Diari 1918*; on the other hand, he observes that he was "betraying this aspiration" when he chose to sign his work with a shortened form of his name, "J. V. Foix." He then concludes, cryptically, that "this *retreat* [*retrocés*] from individual ambition," the youthful decision to withhold his signature, "is only the consequence of the retreat from a collective ambition."

At first sight, this assertion might seem contradictory. One would think that retreating from "individual ambition" might be conducive to joining rather than retreating from a "collective" movement like Catalan nationalism. But the "retreat from a collective ambition" actually refers to a political setback in Catalonia's movement to found a nation: Primo de Rivera's Madrid-backed dictatorship (1923–1930) put an end to the regional commonwealth or Mancommunitat that had been established in 1914 to consolidate the provincial governments in Catalonia and to create cultural institutions like the Institut d'Estudis Catalans to standardize the Catalan language. Consequently, Foix decided to sign his work with his unmistakably Catalan surname, a gesture that was loyal in its ideological force but individualistic as a proper name.

Foix reprinted a revised version of his essay in 1932 as the preface to his second book, *KRTU*. By that point Catalonia had declared itself a republic, and the Generalitat, a political institution dating back to the medieval period, was revived to govern the region. Yet Foix did not revise his sense that a "retreat" had been made. Catalonia had in fact moved forward. Was he not sanguine about recent developments? He suggestively translates "retrocés," the Catalan word for "retreat," with the French "refoulement," the word that Freud's first French translators had chosen to signify the concept of repression. Perhaps for Foix the decision to sign his surrealist texts at once created and repressed an unconscious that was as much political as personal. And perhaps a political unconscious inevitably problematizes an ideology like nationalism by overdetermining it with personal desires. Foix may have seen his recourse to surrealism as a "stylistic elevation" of the Catalan language, as he suggested in his essay "Avant-gardism." But his fantastic images signify further, in excess of that literary nationalism.

* * *

In the first versions of the essay "Some Reflections on One's Own Literature," Foix indicates that the majority of his prose poems have been "transcribed." Although he deleted this remark from later reprints, it reveals that the early fragments of the *Diari 1918* originated as transcriptions of his "psychic states," performed either after his experience of them or from the notebooks where they were recorded. He subsequently destroyed the notebooks, so that determining how extensively the transcriptions were revised before publication remains impossible. Yet in various articles he did provide a basic account of his writing process.

As a surrealist aiming to release and explore the poetic resources of the unconscious, Foix developed a method that favored not automatic writing, freed from rational control, but rather a combination of dream and hypnagogia. The former consists of thoughts, feelings, and sensations that occur in the sleeping mind, the latter of mental phenomena that appear during the transition from waking to sleeping. Foix evidently pursued this method in writing the prose poems he began to publish in 1918, although it was not until 1924 that Breton's *Manifeste du surréalisme* asserted the centrality of dream and hypnagogia to the literary and artistic movement he fostered. "Surrealism," Breton explained, "rests on the belief in the superior reality of certain forms of association hitherto neglected, in the unlimited power of dream, in the disinterested play of thought." He reported a hypnagogic image that has come to typify the movement: before falling asleep one night, he perceived—both verbally and visually—a man cut in two by a window. In 1928 Foix published "Textos Pràctiques" (Practical Texts) in a monthly magazine he coedited, *L'Amic de les Arts*, where he defined more precisely what form such images might take:

> The hypnagogic image is, on some occasions, the *illumination*
> of a word inwardly pronounced or of a figure inwardly evoked.
> On other occasions—and these are of interest—it is the sudden
> irruption of visions, clear, complete, lacking any relation to the
> present course of thought or to some previous performance.

Foix carefully distinguished between dream and hypnagogia in a 1932 article for *La Publicitat*: "Visions are spectacles," he wrote, whereas "dreams give us adventures" in which we are not "spectators," but "actors." As the source of his definitions, he cited Eugène-Bernard Levy's 1926 treatise *Les visions du demi-sommeil: hallucinations hypnagogiques* (The visions of half-sleep: Hypnagogic hallucinations).

Foix's avoidance of the term "hallucination" was deliberate. For him, as for the French surrealists, dream and hypnagogia were visionary, the source of a distinctively poetic knowledge more true than any knowledge that could be acquired through a conscious state of mind. "The precarious external world," Foix stated in a 1933 lecture at the Universitat de Barcelona, "is a deformation of the effective worlds that live in the reality of our dreams." Dream and hypnagogia, according to this view, result in literature characterized by a higher realism that departs from the conventions of verisimilitude. Hence Foix's frequent recourse to the term "superrealism," which he defined in the lecture as the "total negation of external life and exaltation of the fantastic and fundamentally deterministic." The determinism is psychic, the work of the unconscious.

Foix's early fragments unfold a succession of oneiric and hypnagogic images, startling in their juxtaposition and discontinuity, where a narrator, a male voice, is positioned as spectator or actor or both. The images seem to be grounded in Foix's experience insofar they refer to contemporaries within his acquaintance and to locations in Catalonia where he lived or visited. Some of the people and places are explicitly identified or recognizable, while others are transformed beyond recognition. A few female names are cited, Gertrudis repeatedly, but they do not seem to be associated with actual women in Foix's life. Certain images recur to circumscribe a narrow space, bordering on the claustrophobic: a list would include, in ascending order of frequency, fish, shoe, glove, horse, bird, village, square, hand, eye, street, sea. Given their origins in dream and hypnagogia, the images as well as their disposition in a narrative should be regarded as unconsciously motivated, although the nature of the desire they embody or materialize can only be a matter of interpretation.

* * *

Among the patterns that emerge in Foix's early prose poems is a strange contradiction in gender representations. Men, on the one hand, including Foix's first-person narrator, the male subject that focalizes his texts, perform various acts of violence against women, such as decapitation, stabbing, and pushing off a cliff. The violence can also be figurative, enacted through descriptions that reduce women to physical fragments (eyes, lips, breasts, genitalia, legs) or to articles of clothing that are fetishized (shoes, gloves, stockings). The male subject, on the other hand, is at times portrayed as physically and psychologically weak, fainting, awestruck or confused, attempting but unable to engage in sexual intercourse with a woman. Here too the weakness can be figurative, signified in images that invite psychoanalytic readings, such as dead birds and severed feet.

Violence against women is characteristic of surrealist literature and art, but male weakness assuredly is not. In the 1924 manifesto, Breton asserts that "Sade is surrealist in sadism." This aspect of surrealism bears a certain relation to traditions of European love poetry that stretch from antiquity to the early modern period and beyond. In these traditions, the silent woman who is the object of the male poet's desire is never given a coherent, comprehensive representation. She is not only silenced but also represented in part or as a collection of bodily parts, which are occasionally arranged in a sequence that moves from head to toe. Petrarch developed this practice in his descriptions of Laura, whom Foix mentions in a text addressed to Gertrudis, and it quickly became the conventional form known as the "blazon." Although intended to compliment the woman's beauty through idealizing analogies, the blazon amounts to a symbolic dismemberment of her. To dismember the woman allows the poet to maintain his subjective coherence instead of succumbing to the disintegrating force of his desire. The very sign of that coherence is the poem in which she is fragmented. The blazon is thus a defense mechanism wherein the male subject's desire is at the same time expressed and repressed through idealizing images.

Surrealism pushes the dismemberment to an extreme. Whereas the typical Petrarchan form is a sonnet, Breton's 1931 poem "L'Union libre" (Free union) presents a sixty-line description of a silent woman that reduces her to physical fragments whose significance the poet controls. The poem consists of the recurrent formula "Ma femme à," where the preposition "à" signifies her metaphorical possession of various traits. In a rough translation, then, the first line, "Ma femme à la chevelure de feu de bois," might read: "My woman whose hair is a wood fire." Studiously avoiding the flowers, gems, and celestial objects that support the conventional idealization, Breton creates dense, extravagant analogies that are predominantly natural, although dotted with the mechanical and the blasphemous. Here is a revealing extract translated to establish a semantic correspondence:

> My woman whose mouth is a cockade with the
>   fragrance of stars at the utmost luminosity
> Whose teeth are the footprints of white mice on
>   white earth
> Whose tongue is polished amber and glass
> My woman whose tongue is a knifed host
> The tongue of a doll that opens and shuts its eyes
> A tongue of incredible stone
>
>   (ll. 5–10)

Some of the anatomical parts that Breton includes are sexual, while others are not particularly romantic or arousing, even if they are fetishized:

"wrists" ("poignets") as well as "breasts" ("seins"), "belly" ("ventre") as well as "buttocks" ("fesses"), "armpits" ("aiselles") as well as "genitals" ("sexe"). He also associates the woman's body with various forms of violence: "heat lightning" ("éclairs de chaleur"), "the otter's waist in a tiger's teeth" ("la taille de loutre entre les dents du tigre"), "woods always under the ax" ("bois toujours sous la hache"). In the end, "L'Union libre" is basically a blazon designed to disrupt bourgeois morality by going beyond traditional love poetry. Yet it winds up reinforcing rather than revising the convention of constructing male subjective coherence through female dismemberment.

Foix's contradictory representations, in contrast, do enact such a revision by exposing the psychological conditions that underlie surrealism as well as European poetic traditions. His narrator's encounters with Gertrudis are informed by what has come to be known as the madonna-whore complex. In the 1912 essay "On the Universal Tendency to Debasement in the Sphere of Love," Freud provides a succinct formulation: "Where they [men] love they do not desire and where they desire they cannot love." The men who exhibit this complex are unable to reconcile affectionate love with sexual desire: love for a woman entails idealization that causes impotence, whereas desire presupposes debasement that enables consummation. In Foix's representations, however, Gertrudis is treated as *both* madonna and whore, provoking an equally divided reaction from the narrator, both adoration and lust. Thus she entertains a number of lovers and wears a red dress to taunt him. But she is also a devout churchgoer who takes notes on sermons, and she is depicted as sitting on a silver throne, attended by angelic figures. The narrator, in turn, wounds a rival for her love in a duel and makes sexual advances toward her. But he also fetishizes her shoe and her gloves and fails to perform sexually. These contradictions, distributed over a series of prose poems, are never reconciled.

If Foix's early fragments are read against an anti-blazon like Breton's "L'Union libre," they might be seen as a gender critique of French surrealism. Foix's treatment of Gertrudis shows that, far from releasing the unconscious, Breton's metaphorical dismemberment of the woman represses the conditions of the male subject's desire. "L'Union libre" is clearly presented as an idealization, a catalogue of unconventional compliments that fit the subversive aspirations of surrealism, but they actually debase the woman, and it is her debasement that elicits male desire.

Foix's writing remains complicit in the gender representations that it seems to question. Any critique that might be perceived is still staged through images of a woman subordinated to a male subject. Yet by interrogating surrealist forms and practices, Foix upsets a different hierarchy, not the inequality between genders but the global ranking of national cultures—namely, the uneven distribution of cultural prestige and resources that existed between French and Catalan literatures in the early twentieth century. His dependence on surrealism implicitly acknowledges the minority of the Catalan language in relation to a major language like French, which had accumulated literary capital for centuries before modernism increased it further. Yet the remarkably inventive way in which Foix puts to work surrealist materials challenges French dominance while producing a Catalan achievement that ultimately takes a place in the world literary scene.

* * *

Foix's first two books immediately attracted the attention of Catalan reviewers, but the reviewers' opinions were sharply divided. His modernist experimentalism, not surprisingly, elicited negative judgments from those who revered traditional literary forms and practices. As a result, although Foix's affiliation with surrealism was recognized as a matter of course, little effort was made to understand not just that his writing was unconsciously motivated but that its significance might be grasped with the use of psychoanalytic concepts. Domènec Guansé, a realistic novelist who translated Prévost, Balzac, and Maupassant into Catalan, reviewed *Gertrudis* for the highbrow monthly *Revista de Catalunya*, describing the work as "a fugue of nearly incoherent sentences" that "do not awaken any ideas in the brain." For Guansé, the key to literary success was immediate intelligibility, not the application of recent research in a field like psychology. Foix's writing was therefore meaningless to him. "What good are images," he asked, "if they are not signs of an idea?"

As Guansé's remarks suggest, Foix was criticized for failing to take proper control of his reader's response. He invited interpretation, although within certain conceptual parameters; the reviewers preferred that any interpretation be limited or entirely preempted. The acerbic poet and playwright Joan Oliver, reviewing *Gertrudis* for the conservative *Diari de Sabadell*, complained that Foix's "manner of distancing the reader" permitted "only a purely sensory artistic spectacle" such that "intrinsic meaning" was abandoned to "the varied, capricious possibilities of a personal hermeneutic."

Oliver assumed that "profound literary value" inheres in the author's communication of an intended meaning, whereas Foix's "intentions," in his view, "will remain increasingly ignored in the world like a nun completely cloistered." To Manuel de Montoliu, however, a *Modernista* poet who subsequently became a noted literary historian, Foix's intentions were all too clear; they were just wrong. In reviewing *KRTU* for *La Veu de Catalunya*, Montoliu observed that the author's role "is reduced to making new combinations, new complexes of the same sensations that we receive from the material world," so that the reader "does not transcend to the world of art, in which there must be a constant transformation of sensation into imagination and imagination into spirit." In this case, Foix's writing was faulted because it did not display an advocacy of idealist aesthetics.

La Publicitat, where Foix was a regular contributor, ran two positive reviews of *Gertrudis*, although neither reviewer seemed much interested in Foix's surrealism. Tomàs Garcés, a poet who modeled his work on the Catalan folk song, confessed that "it is pointless to search for a narrative, such as we understand the word." The novelist Carles Soldevila performed his role as *Noucentista* popularizer by casting his piece as an interview with "the ingenuous reader" who needs to be educated about Foix's project. But Soldevila was more disposed to backhanded compliment than incisive commentary. "This literary somnambulism," he explained,

> still demands a strong dose of intelligence; when all is said and done, the super-realist poet or narrator does not renounce waking up at particular moments and throwing a quick, invisible punch. . . . That is to say, he doesn't renounce cheating.

Both reviewers seized the opportunity to claim Foix's achievement for Catalanism by contesting the authority of the French surrealists. Garcés believed Foix to be their "precursor," dating his "fantastic daybook" to a period "long before Breton launched his famous manifesto in France and even long before Freud's theories might have interested any man of letters." Soldevila simply advised his reader that there wasn't "the slightest need to envy André Breton or Benjamin Peret."

By far the most perceptive review of *Gertrudis* came from Lluís Montanyà, who coedited *L'Amic de les Arts* with Foix and actively promoted the avant-garde movements in Catalonia. Writing for the trendy cosmopolitan monthly *La Nova Revista*, Montanyà demonstrated his broad familiarity with Foix's writing through quotations from material that had appeared in periodicals or was still unpublished. Montanyà's opening gambit was a Futurist-like equation that factored in Foix's various influences, although Breton was conspicuously absent:

Dream + lyricism + subconscious + intuition + relativity + rhetoric + introspection + subjective logic + influences and/or coincidences: Reverdy-Einstein, Max-Jacob-Freud = Avant-gardism? Romanticism? Classicism? = A neo-Romantic Classicizing Avant-gardist = J. V. FOIX.

By "classicizing" Montanyà had in mind Foix's interest in traditional literary forms as well as his style, which was called "perfect—a model of Catalan prose, purified, enriched, ennobled." This sort of praise rested on the same vernacular nationalism that made Foix wary of how avant-garde practices used indiscriminately could derail the development of the Catalan language. Hence Montanyà was careful to add that Foix's prose "situates him among the greatest stylists and reformers of our idiom." His examples were two leading *Noucentista* poets, Josep Carner and Carles Riba.

The reviews indicate that Catalan readers were gradually developing the ability to comprehend Foix's difficult work, regardless of their literary tastes. The *Noucentista* poet Rossend Llates, reviewing *KRTU* for the arts-and-politics weekly *Mirador*, deciphered "the identity between the titles of Foix's two books," whereby "the second seems to be a geometric stylization of the first." Guillem Díaz-Plaja, a literary historian who authored the 1932 study *L'avantguardisme a Catalunya*, contributed what appears to be the first critical essay on Foix's writing to *La Publicitat*. Concentrating on features like meter and rhyme scheme, Díaz-Plaja argued that traditional forms structure Foix's prose so that the rhythms of the late medieval folk song known as the "corranda" are juxtaposed to the "agility of a Futurist poem in the manner of Guillaume Apollinaire." These prosodic effects, moreover, are consistent with Foix's surrealist practices, resulting in what Díaz-Plaja termed "derived creation." "In the purity of complete unconsciousness," he explained, "you will find seams of consciousness, of reason, of memory. The word clangs methodically, and the poet draws music or suggestion from it."

* * *

Foix's writing achieved canonical status during his lifetime, first in Catalonia but eventually elsewhere as well. In 1961 he was elected to the Philological Section of the Institut d'Estudis Catalans, an academy limited to twenty-eight participating members who oversee the development of the Catalan language. He received a number of regional and national awards for his writing—from Spain (1966, 1984), the Generalitat of Catalonia (1973, 1981), and the city of Barcelona (1980). In 1984 France named him a Chevalier de l'Ordre des Arts et des Lettres.

This recognition attests to the increasingly lenient enforcement of Franco's repressive language policies, which elevated Castilian over Catalan as well as the other regional languages of Spain. Yet until the regime ended in 1975, even a canonical writer might feel the need to anticipate censorship. Thus in 1969, when Foix included "Homeland" in a collection of his articles for *La Publicitat*, he revised the initial 1935 version by removing points that the Franquistas might find objectionable. He deleted an account of totalitarian states as "destroying the meaning of individuality," and he substituted "conservative" for "rightist" in describing a segment of the press.

Meanwhile, as befitted a figure who had acquired considerable symbolic and cultural capital, Foix was inspiring a flood of secondary material in various languages. From the 1950s to the 1980s this material included interviews and critical editions, research monographs and journal articles, conference proceedings and anniversary volumes. The year 1952 saw the first Castilian translation of Foix's poetry. In 1958 the first doctoral thesis to address his work was defended at the Universitat de Barcelona. In the 1960s, anthology selections were translated into Brazilian Portuguese, Dutch, and Italian, and by the 1980s, book-length translations had appeared in French, German, and English. The translations currently encompass sixteen languages, including Chinese, Hungarian, Japanese, Slovenian, and Turkish.

Anglophone cultures have been less hospitable to Foix, partly because the global dominance of English has led to their aggressive monolingualism and partly because the minority of Catalan simultaneously limits and demands the cultural knowledge necessary for an informed appreciation. Not unexpectedly, then, it is primarily academics who have expressed admiration. Peter Cocozzella, professor of Spanish literatures at the State University of New York at Binghamton, reviewed the 1981 edition of the *Diari 1918* for *World Literature Today*, noting the resemblances to the work of writers like Louis Aragon, Breton, and Éluard. Yet Cocozzella particularly valued the "deft interplay of international and local currents" in Foix's brand of surrealism, emphasizing "the author's uncanny talent for anchoring even the most experimental, art-for-art's-sake, avant-gardist flights of his imagination in vivid, veristic details, evidenced in his constant reliance upon character sketches drawn from lifelike Catalan types, upon backdrop descriptions inspired by authentic Catalan land- and seascapes, upon idioms and lexicon reflecting exuberant manifestations of Catalan speech."

In *The Western Canon* (1994), Harold Bloom ventured to predict that Foix would be installed in a modernist pantheon that includes Freud and Proust, Joyce and Woolf, Kafka and Beckett. Bloom's criteria had nothing to do with "cultural politics of any kind," whether in Catalonia or in the United States, but only with "aesthetic" qualities that reflect the "literary spirit" of the twentieth century, which he dubbed "The Chaotic Age." This estimation has undoubtedly contributed to Foix's international reception, but in excluding his distinctively Catalan significance, Bloom encouraged a response that is culturally and historically impoverished.

Anglophone translators and publishers have generally neglected Foix's writing. Only one book-length selection has been published in English: David Rosenthal's 1988 translation, which was issued by the small New York press Persea and is long out of print. This selection contains thirty-five texts, including four excerpts from *Gertrudis* and *KRTU*. Rosenthal was a prolific translator of Catalan literature who published poetry anthologies and undertook such canonical works as Martorell and Galba's *Tirant lo Blanc* and the prose fiction of Victor Català (the pseudonym of Caterina Albert), Joan Perucho, Joan Sales, and Mercé Rodoreda. Here is his version of an early fragment from the *Diari 1918*:

> When I spied my rival in the distance, motionlessly awaiting me on the beach, I wondered if it was him, my horse, or Gertrude. As I approached, I realized it was a stone phallus, gigantic, erected in the far-off past. Its shadow covered half the sea and an indecipherable legend was inscribed at the base. I went closer so I could copy it, but before me, lying open on the burning sand, was only my umbrella. Upon the sea, without shadow of ships or clouds, floated those enormous gloves worn by the mysterious monster who chased you toward evening beneath the Ribera's plane trees.

Rosenthal's work is accomplished. His lexicon and syntax follow current standard English so closely that the slightest deviations are noticeable, like the shift to a more poetical register with "spied," "before me," and "upon the sea." Most of the language is quite common, in fact, verging on colloquial, words and phrases like "wondered," "if it was" (instead of the more formal subjunctive, "were"), "went closer," and "chased." He also anglicizes "Gertrudis" as "Gertrude." The result of these choices is eminent readability, a fluency that makes the text accessible and engaging. Hence, in what seems to be the only review of Rosenthal's Foix translation, the poet and novelist Jana Harris gravitates toward the "short selection of gem-like prose poems" while dismissing the excerpts from Foix's other major works, *Sol, i de dol* and *Les irreals omegues*, as "on the whole unremarkable," even "somewhat vague and less than memorable." Rosenthal's type of fluent translation, adhering closely to standard linguistic items that are immediately familiar and thus easy to process, may have abetted the superficiality of Harris's response. Her conclusion devolves into utter cliché: Foix's prose poems, she writes, demonstrate that "his rightful place in literary history" is to "line up behind the work of Breton and Apollinaire."

* * *

To translate, to rewrite a text so that it is intelligible and interesting in a different language and culture, is a decontextualizing move. The source text is unavoidably—some would say necessarily—detached from the diverse contexts that make it uniquely meaningful, valuable, and functional in the culture where it originated. These contexts comprise patterns of linguistic usage, cultural traditions and conventions, literary forms and practices, a spectrum of values, beliefs, and representations, and various modes of reception, both in print and electronic media and in social institutions.

Consequently, translation makes possible a reading experience that differs markedly from the experience of a reader with access to the source text, especially since the source-language reader may well possess a broad and deep familiarity with the source culture. This disjunction is increased with a minor language and literature like Catalan, since minority means marginality, defined by narrow circulation and restricted knowledge in relation to whatever stands for a major language and literature, a cultural center. No wonder, then, that readers, confronted with a translation, fall back on what they know and prefer: they read and evaluate the translation mainly against linguistic patterns, literary practices, and cultural values in the receiving situation, which is usually the culture that they call their own, whether because it is native or because they experience it as primary.

These considerations assumed special importance as I developed my translation of Foix's writing. The editorial work, which involved not only the selection and arrangement of the Catalan texts but also the supplementary materials such as this introduction and the notes—this work served to construct a multifaceted context *in English* designed to enhance the reader's comprehension. I followed Foix's own editing of the *Diari 1918* in choosing to establish the early fragments as the center of the project. Despite their fragmentary quality, they possess a remarkable coherence that becomes richly suggestive when they are read together. The bilingual format, furthermore, can drive the reader deeper not just into the source texts but also into the translations while insisting on the very fact that the source language is Catalan, a language rather than a dialect, autonomous and distinct from, if related to, Castilian and other Romance languages.

The recontextualizing process continued in the assembly of two other groups of texts. Because many of the early fragments appeared in *Gertrudis* and *KRTU*, I have included translations of the other work that Foix published in those first two books, a varied assortment of poetry in verse and in prose, along with prose fictions, a lyrical letter, and narrative portraits of Catalan painters. Not only do these translations make available a wider sampling of Foix's writing from the same period, they offer a glimpse of how he imagined the early fragments as a discrete body of work with a definite form and a coherent set of themes. I have also included translations of several essays in which Foix discusses his own writing, responds to the modernist avant-garde movements in Europe, surveys current trends in Catalan art and literature, and comments on international political developments. These essays add a historical dimension to the literary texts, serving as a reminder that Foix was actively intervening into a cultural and political situation that is now more than a century old. Nonetheless, the issues that engaged him then, notably the question of Catalan nationalism, can also contribute to a history of the present insofar as they inevitably bear on Catalonia's ongoing struggle for independence.

My overall strategy in translating Foix's powerful synthesis of international modernism, particularly surrealism, with Catalan traditions and locales was to maintain a semantic correspondence that approximates the stylistic features of his writing, its periodic structures and rhythms. In

English this strategy sometimes led to greater formality and poetical archaism, even though the translation draws mostly on the current standard dialect. My language is heterogeneous, in other words, so as to enrich the reader's response. The formal, archaizing tendency can suggest the historical remoteness of Foix's texts while heightening the more colloquial elements as well as the surrealist imagery. Foix's surrealism can seem stranger in my English than in his Catalan, which is rather homogeneous.

Readability remained a primary goal throughout, but so did literary effect. Assuming that Foix's work should be just as resonant in English as in Catalan, I have written translations to be read as literary texts in their own right. The crucial word "diari," for instance, can be rendered simply as "diary." But Foix's "diari" was actually a journal that functioned as a laboratory for literary experiment, not just as a collection of personal reflections and autobiographical narratives. I chose "daybook" because it joins the sense of daily entries with more literary connotations: the term "daybook" has been used by such important United States poets as George Oppen, Robert Duncan, Robert Creeley, and Marilyn Hacker to indicate a form that variously combines features of a journal, memoir, work in progress, even a cluster of finished poems. Implying a likeness to poets of their stature is also a means of alluding to Foix's canonical position in Catalan literature for readers who have limited access to the language and culture.

If anglophone readers lacking Catalan—the audience I most hope to reach—are likely to respond to the translations by relying on English-language traditions and trends, how might Foix's writing be gauged against the poetry scenes in cultures like the United States and the United Kingdom? His poetics uncannily resembles the "reigning style" that Stephen (now Stephanie) Burt called "elliptical" in the late 1990s, but that since then has seemed to describe an ever-widening stream of contemporary poetry. In Burt's account, this style is characterized by "fragmentation, jumpiness, audacity; performance, grammatical oddity; rebellion, voice, some measure of closure." And just as Foix tapped surrealism to depict Catalan culture, Burt's elliptical poets "split the difference between a poetry of descriptive realism on the one hand and, on the other, a neo-avant-garde." Burt's examples include August Kleinzahler and Susan Wheeler, Dean Young and Claudia Rankine, Mark Levine and Matthea Harvey—poets who are still quite productive, whose work is reviewed widely, and who have received distinguished awards. He also mentions at least one British poet: Mark Ford.

Any resemblance between these poets and Foix foregrounds irreducible differences, which can in turn initiate a critical dialectic where each questions the other. The elliptical habit of "laying down a series of hints, or residues, of experience," as Burt describes it, and of rejecting "poems written in order to demonstrate theories" highlights Foix's quite different approach of recurrently deploying psychoanalytic symbols with fairly fixed meanings. At the same time, Foix's cosmopolitan Freudianism discloses the absence of a philosophical code in the anglophone poets, their recourse to literary or rhetorical figures to generate meaning in an English-language context. Translation interprets, never simply reproduces or transfers, and the interpretations that it makes possible can trouble the translating culture as well as the source text, although only for the suspicious reader who is also inclined to be self-conscious. Perhaps now is the moment to release Foix's interrogative power in English, challenging a century of neglect.

Joan Miró, Drawing for J.V. Foix, *Gertrudis*, 1927.

Joan Miró, "Drawing for an Object," in J.V. Foix, *KRTU*, 1932.

Early Fragments from the Daybook

In 1981 J. V. Foix gathered prose poems that he had been printing in magazines and in individual book-length selections over the preceding half century, a total of 203, and he published them under the title *Diari 1918* (*Daybook 1918*). He grouped the earliest texts in the first section, which he titled "Primers fragments del Diari" (Early Fragments from the Daybook). These texts, forty-five in all, constitute the basis of the translations presented here with Foix's Catalan *en face*. The sequence of texts as well as the titles follow Foix's editing.

Diari 1918 (Fragments)

A la memòria de Joaquim Folguera

He malferit en duel el teu amant. Però perquè duus el vestit carmesí, te'n rius. I perquè, amb la teva perfídia, has substituït l'amant pel tramoista. Jo puniria la teva malifeta si el perruquer no hagués estat el teu còmplice en desfigurar-me grotescament la faç. Un altre bell matí, però, em venjaré. El sostre ni serà, com ara, tan i tan baix, ni hi haurà pintats, com ara, tants d'ocells morts.

Daybook 1918 (Fragments)

I wounded your lover gravely in a duel. Yet you mock the incident by wearing the crimson dress. And by replacing the lover, deceitfully, with the scene-shifter at the theatre. I would punish your misdeeds if the barber had not been your accomplice in disfiguring my face so grotesquely. On another fine morning, however, I will take my revenge. The ceiling will not be, as now, so very low, nor will so many dead birds, as now, be painted on it.

Aixequeu ben alts els murs del meu carrer. Tan alts que, en ésser nit, no hi entri ni la remor de les fontanes ni el xiscle agònic de les locomotrius. Feu que el meu carrer tingui tot just l'amplada de la meva passa. No feu obertures als murs, i arrieu del cim de les torratxes tantes de banderes i de gallardets. Doneu-me només el goig que, a trenc d'alba, del pas de l'ombra de la meva amada a mitjanit en resti el testimoni d'una flor vermella marcint-se a la penombra, o d'una sabata esberlada flotant damunt un toll.

Raise high the walls of my street. Let them tower so high that at nightfall neither the murmur of the fountains nor the agonizing shriek of the trains might enter. See to it that my street measures the very width of my step. Form no openings in the walls, and lower every flag and pennant from the tops of the turrets. Grant me no more than the joy that remains at daybreak after my beloved's shadow has passed at midnight, the testimony of a red flower withering in the dimness, or a crushed shoe floating on the surface of a puddle.

M'assegurava que eren dos-cents els joves del poble que tenien un cavall negre com el meu. Però vaig espiar, una a una, llurs estables i vaig comprovar el seu engany. Les estables són buides i són buides les cases. Al poble només hi som jo i el meu cavall que errem de nit i de dia pel laberint de les seves ombres. Quant a Gertrudis, és ben morta al fons de l'abisme on la vaig precipitar. O és que tants de milers d'estels que guspiregen en la negror celeste no exalten la joia de la meva solitud?

She assured me that two hundred young men lived in the village, each the owner of a black horse like mine. But I scrutinized their stables, one by one, and I exposed her ruse. The stables lie empty, as do the houses. Only my horse and I wander the village, night and day, through the labyrinth of its shadows. As for Gertrudis, she lies dead at the foot of the abyss where I hurled her headlong. Or is it that so many thousands of stars glittering in the celestial blackness fail to exalt the joy of my solitude?

Quants de tombs jo havia dat adés per l'exterior dels murs de la catedral bastida dalt el pujol! Aleshores anaves al temple cada dia, cenyit el front de roses, a prendre notes taquigràfiques del sermó de les Set Paraules. Jo, mentrestant, arrossegant un piano de maneta, cercava, àvid, els aparadors on hi havia exposades les divines sabates de xarol o els meravellosos paraigües, invenció dels homes. M'han dit que havies reprès el vell costum i que tornaves cada dia al temple. Però en anar-me-n'hi avui, el temple havia desaparegut i al seu lloc, immensament deserta, hi havia, en vidre policrom, una estàtua del meu cavall, que centellejava en tènues rosasses als flancs del pujol.

How many times have I strolled around the walls of that cathedral built on the hill! In those days, your brow wreathed with roses, you would frequent the temple daily to take shorthand notes on the sermon about Christ's last seven words. I, meanwhile, trailing along a barrel organ, eagerly sought shop windows that displayed divine patent leather shoes and marvelous umbrellas, the invention of men. They told me you had resumed the ancient custom, returning to the temple every day. Yet today when I arrived there, the temple had disappeared, and in its place, vastly deserted, stood a statue of my horse in polychrome glass, gleaming in the faint rose windows of the hillsides.

Diuen que estàs gelosa de la gropa de la noia de la lletera. Però he estat a casa seva i he vist la consola amb el mirall on se pentina. A les pregoneses del mirall, dues amples cortines vermelloses cobricelaven l'entrada a un passadís al fons del qual hi havia un quadre. Una vella litografia hi representava les tortures a què el diable sotmet les noies que, en tornant de sarau, a mitjanit, es contemplen al mirall. M'ha torbat tant, que he tardat a adonar-me que el marc del mirall i el marc de l'entrada al passadís no eren sinó el bastiment de l'entrada a l'establa on senyoreja la gropa del meu cavall.

They say you are jealous of the milkmaid's rump. Even so, I visited her home and saw the mirrored console where she brushes her hair. In the depths of the mirror, two broad ruddy curtains canopy the entrance to a corridor, at the back of which hangs a picture. An ancient lithograph represents the tortures that the devil inflicts upon girls who return from balls at midnight only to contemplate themselves in a mirror. It distracted me so much I was slow to notice: the frames of mirror and corridor were nothing but the frame of the stable door ruled by my horse's rump.

Et vaig sorprendre quan el teu nou amant et donava un estoig magnífic. No era, però, un estoig: era un llibre; ni era tampoc el teu amant ans jo mateix que et regalava una capsa de tubs d'aquarel·la amb les colors de l'iris.

I caught you unawares when your new lover gave you a magnificent box. It was not, however, a box: it was a book. Nor was it your lover but I myself who presented you with a box of watercolors in the spectrum of the rainbow.

Les parets del *court* eren, aquest matí, tan altes que m'han fet oblidar el fiacre on tu m'esperaves, i els ocells. Intentava d'amidar-les, quan s'hi han obert quatre finestrals, de cinc metres, closos per llances en totes direccions. Un perfum intensíssim de paper d'Armènia ha envaït la pista mentre una mà invisible escrivia un nom damunt cada obertura: Ofèlia, Virgínia, Laura, Julieta. Quan anava a reprendre el partit, el meu company de joc havia desaparegut i de la meva raqueta en restava només l'ombra estrafeta, allargassada entre les dues ales fosques de l'angle del mur. A l'entrada del club, el fiacre, sense cavalleria ni auriga, sense tu, oh Gertrudis!, era la desferra secular d'una antiga carrossa reial.

The court walls were so high, this morning, that they made me forget the carriage where you were waiting for me, as well as the birds. I endeavored to measure the walls when four windows opened, each five meters tall, enclosed by lances on every side. A most intense scent of *papier d'Arménie* invaded the path while an invisible hand inscribed a name over each opening: Ophelia, Virginie, Laura, Juliet. When I went to resume the match, my tennis mate had disappeared, and only the deformed shadow of my racquet remained, lengthening between the dark wings at the corner of the wall. At the entrance of the club, the carriage, with neither steed nor charioteer, without you—Getrudis!—stood the century-old wreckage of an ancient royal coach.

Que hagin aparedat portals i finestres; que dalt de la torre no onegin banderes; que les algues en créixer monstruoses cloguin els passatges; que els arbres per damunt els murs s'estenguin en rares floracions vermelles i que tots els carrers donin a la mar abocats en esculls temibles; que els cavalls siguin amos i senyors de la meva vila i s'hi passegin impúdicament nus; que els ocells s'occeixin en topar amb el cel arran de sostre; que el cel sigui només un trist miratge de la mar. Què em pot sorprendre si avui he vist saltar de cop els lloms dels meus llibres i he descobert la putrefacció cancerosa que destrossa llurs entranyes?

May doors and windows be walled up. May no flags fly above the tower. May seaweed grow monstrously and block passageways. May trees spread strange vermilion blossoms over walls, and may every street give onto the sea, headed for fearsome reefs. May horses be lords and masters of my village and saunter through it shamelessly naked. May birds be slain in crashing against the sky close to the ceiling. May the sky be no more than a sad mirage of the sea. What can surprise me if today I saw the spines of my books suddenly fly off, and I discovered the cancerous putrefaction that destroys their entrails?

En percebre de lluny el meu rival que m'esperava, immòbil, a la platja, he dubtat si era ell o el meu cavall o Gertrudis. En acostar-m'hi, m'he adonat que era un fal·lus de pedra, gegantí, erigit en edats pretèrites. Cobria amb la seva ombra mitja mar i duia gravada al sòcol una llegenda indesxifrable. M'he acotat per a copiar-la, però al meu davant, badat en ple sorral ardent, hi havia únicament el meu paraigua. Damunt la mar, sense ombra de vaixell ni de núvol, suraven els guants enormes que calça el monstre misteriós que et persegueix cap al tard sota els plàtans de la Ribera.

Upon perceiving my rival in the distance, motionless, waiting for me on the beach, I could not be certain whether it was he, my horse, or Gertrudis. Drawing near, I realized that it was a stone phallus, gigantic, erected in past epochs. Its shadow covered half of the sea, and it bore an indecipherable legend engraved on the plinth. I stooped to copy it, but before me stood only my umbrella, opened in the midst of the burning sand. On the sea, devoid of shadow from boat or cloud, floated an enormous pair of gloves. They fit the mysterious monster who pursues you at dusk beneath the plane trees of the Ribera.

Per a Carles Riba

Quan érem a la font tots dos, un missatger del rei m'ha dit que hi havia guerra. He pres la meva arma, i l'home de la carota de gegant no em vol deixar passar. En allargar-li tu una flor, havia desaparegut. Tu no li donaves, però, una flor sinó la meva arma amb la qual m'hauria pogut occir. On és l'arma? On és la flor? A l'home de la carota de gegant l'he vist avui penjat al portal de la Seu de Manresa fent una ganyota agònica. Però al fons del gorg de les seves pupil·les t'he vist a tu amb la flor als llavis i l'arma al braç. Per què m'has deixat, Gertrudis?

When we were standing together by the spring, a messenger of the king told me that war had broken out. I seized my weapon, and the man, who had a *gegant*'s droll face, would not let me pass. As you held out a flower to him, it disappeared. Yet you gave him, not a flower, but my weapon, with which he could have slain me. Where is the weapon? Where the flower? Today I glimpsed the man with the face of a *gegant* hanging in the portal of the Seu de Manresa, grimacing in agony. Deep in the pools of his pupils, however, I saw you with the flower at your lips and the weapon in your hand. Why have you abandoned me, Gertrudis?

A les sis de la tarda—i no a les dotze de la nit—havíem arrambat els basti-
dors polsosos a la cantonada perquè allarguessin llur ombra morada a tot
el carrer. Què hi feia aquella cadira Lluís XV al portal de ca l'espardenyer?
Els pàl·lids apotecaris havien penjat distrets els globus de porcellana, enter-
anyinats, al portal de les barberies i els perruquers amb sabates de cimolsa
s'havien posat les carotes que pengen, a entrada de fosc, sota els balcons
i s'amagaven per les escaletes. Les persianes de totes les finestres s'havien
obert horitzontalment: al fons de cada alcova una corrua d'ombres dibui-
xava, en rastre fosforescent, paisatges bíblics. Una gran cortina vermella
penjava de cap a cap del carrer on vaig intentar inútilment d'amagar el
maniquí de la cotillaire. M'havien dit que a darrere la cortina hi eres tu
assajant una nova atracció de circ; però la cortina dissimulava només el
mur altíssim que tanca els jardins hipotètics del gran castell on la lluna
es dissol, cada nit, en piperitina. Vaig trucar, sense eco, a totes les cases;
vaig seguir, en va, el túnel de l'un cap a l'altre. Però a les set, quan anava
a plànyer-me de la meva dissort a la penombra de l'establa, vaig descobrir,
a la rebotiga del foll d'En Miquel, sota la claror clandestina d'un quinqué,
l'amo, amb la teva testa decapitada a la mà on emprovava arrissades per-
ruques subversives.

At six in the afternoon—not twelve at night—we laid the dusty frames against the corner so that they might cast their violet shadow over the entire street. What was that Louis XV armchair doing at the espadrille maker's door? The pale apothecaries had absentmindedly hung the cobweb-covered porcelain globes at the entrances to the barber shops. The wig makers in their woolen slippers had clapped on the grotesque masks that dangle beneath the balconies at nightfall, and then they hid from view by the stairs. The blinds of every window had been opened horizontally: at the back of each alcove, a row of shadows sketched biblical landscapes in phosphorescent traces. A huge red curtain was draped the length of the street where to no avail I tried to conceal the corset maker's mannequin. They had told me that behind the curtain you would be rehearsing a new circus attraction, but the curtain hid only a very high wall enclosing the hypothetical gardens of the great castle where the moon dissolves, every night, in piperidine. I called, without response, at every house; I followed the tunnel, in vain, from one end to the other. At seven, however, when I went off to moan about my misfortune in the gloom of the stable, I discovered the proprietor in mad Miquel's back room, under the stealthy light of an oil lamp, holding your severed head, where he was trying on several subversively curled wigs.

Les cases, de roure i de caoba, s'enfilaven turó amunt i formaven una piràmide caprici d'un artífex ebenista. Aquell era el poble on, sota el signe d'Escorpió, sojornava Gertrudis. Eren tan drets els carrers, que em creia, abans d'ésser al cim, defallir. De l'interior de les cases sortien rares músiques com d'un estoig de cigars harmònic. El cel, de pur cristall, es podia tocar amb les mans. Blava, vermella, verda o groga, cada casa tenia hissada la seva bandera. Si no hagués anat carregat d'un feixuc bidó de vernís, inelegant, m'hauria estret més el nus de la corbata. Al capdamunt del carrer més ample, al vèrtex mateix del turó, sota una cortina blau cel, seia, en un tron d'argent, Gertrudis. Totes vestides de blau cel també, les noies lliscaven, alades, amunt i avall dels carrers, i feien com si no em veiessin. Cenyien el cabell amb un llaç escocès i descobrien els portals i les finestres on vidrieres de fosques colors innombrables donaven al carrer el recolliment de l'interior d'una catedral submergida a la claror de les rosasses. El grinyol del calçat em semblava un cor dolcíssim, i la meva ombra esporuguia l'ombra dels ocells presoners de l'ampla claraboia celeste. Quan em creia d'atènyer el cim, dec haver errat la passa: em trobava en el tebi passadís interminable d'un vaixell transatlàntic. M'han mancat forces per cridar i, en cloure'm la por els ulls, desplegada en ventall, una sèrie completa de cartes de joc em mostrava inimaginables paisatges desolats.

The houses of oak and mahogany climbed the hill, forming the whimsical pyramid of an artful carpenter. That was the village where, under the sign of Scorpio, Gertrudis made her sojourn. The streets were so steep that I thought I would weaken before reaching the top. From inside the houses issued a strange music as from a harmonic box of cigars. A sky of pure crystalline could be touched by the hand. Each house hoisted its flag, blue, red, green, or yellow. If I had not been burdened by a heavy, inelegant can of varnish, I would have tightened the knot in my tie. At the top of the widest street, at the very summit of the hill, beneath a sky-blue curtain, sat Gertrudis on a silver throne. Girls were gliding up and down the streets, bewinged, all dressed in sky blue as well, and they acted as if they had not seen me. Their hair was encircled by a Scotch bow. They pointed out doors and windows where glasswork in countless deep hues endowed the street with the seclusion of a cathedral immersed in the light of rose windows. The squeak of a shoe seemed like the sweetest choir to me, and my shadow frightened the shadow of the birds, prisoners of the wide celestial skylight. When I thought I had reached the top, I must have lost my way: I found myself in the warm interminable passageway of a transatlantic vessel. I lacked the strength to cry out, and as I closed my eyes in fear, a complete deck of playing cards, spread out into a fan, opened landscapes before me, unimaginable and desolate.

La vila

La meva vila és sobre una plataforma circular. Totes les cases donen per llurs portals a la plaça i, perpendiculars, els deu carrers sense sortida. Al mig de la plaça, alta de cent metres, s'alça una torre mil·lenària sense cap obertura. Al cim oneja una bandera negra teixida d'estels retallats de paper d'argent. No sap hom de ningú que hagi anat més enllà de la plaça i tothom ignora què hi ha més enllà dels murs que tanquen els carrers. No cal dir com de segle en segle augmenten les llegendes que fan més paorosa l'existència exterior. El cel del meu poble, com els gonfanons del Via Crucis, té de nit i de dia, immòbils, el sol, la lluna i els estels, pàl·lidament lluminosos. En desvetllar-nos, tots els joves del poble muntem les bicicletes i, a grans tocs de botzina, desvetllem el veïnat. Les noies treuen les cadires als portals i s'hi asseuen. Miren tendrament com els joves fem les nostres curses al voltant de la plaça, i es cobreixen el pit de medalles perquè guanyi llur amic. Tots portem brodat al jersei, amb fil de seda de colors, el nom de l'estimada. Acabades les curses deixem els bicicles recolzats a la torre i anem a seure a costat del nostre amor. Ens donem les mans, i així passem hores i hores. Les mares obren els balcons i hi estenen els domassos.

En acostar-se l'hora del repòs, en un angle de la plaça s'obre una trapa i enmig d'una fumerola d'encens surt el pare Fèlix. Porta tot de llibres sota un braç i es passa l'altra mà per la barbassa. I diu, un dia:—Déu es dóna sempre tot. Mai no dóna un braç, o una galta, o una cama. Ni mai no dóna un braç a un altre braç, o una galta a una altra galta, ni una cama a una altra cama. I, un altre dia, diu:—La nostra vila és un acte d'amor de Déu, i totes les coses són filles de l'amor. Aleshores ens mirem llargament als ulls i estrenyem més les mans amoroses.

The Village

My village sits on a circular platform. The front door of every house faces toward the square and stands perpendicular to ten streets, all culs-de-sac. In the center of the square, one hundred meters high, rises an ancient tower without any opening. At the top flies a black flag woven with stars cut from silver paper. No one has gone beyond the square, and no one knows what lies beyond the walls that close off the streets. Needless to say, the legends that represent life outside as more frightening increase from century to century. Night and day the sky of my town, like the gonfalons of the Via Crucis, holds sun, moon, and stars motionless and palely luminous. When we young people awake, we ride bicycles and wake the neighborhood with loud trumpet blares. Girls bring chairs to the doors of their homes and sit there. They watch tenderly as we ride our races round and round the square, and they cover their chests with medals so their beaus might win. We all wear jerseys embroidered with our darlings' names in colored thread. When the races are finished, we prop up our bicycles against the tower and go sit at the sides of our loves. We hold hands and spend hours on end like this. Mothers open their balconies and lay out their damasks.

As the hour of rest draws near, a trapdoor opens in a corner of the square, and in the midst of a cloud of incense appears the priest, Father Felix. He carries a stack of books under his arm and runs his other hand through his long beard. One day he says: "God always gives himself whole to us. Never does he give one arm or one cheek or one leg. Nor does he ever give an arm to another arm, or a cheek to another cheek, or a leg to another leg." Another day he says: "Our village is an act of God's love, and all things are love's offspring." At that moment, we look at length into each other's eyes, and we again grasp amorous hands.

27

Fra Fèlix, entre una nova fumerola d'encens, se'n torna pel cotilló, carregat amb les bicicletes. El cel, amb el sol, la lluna i els estels, es mou suaument com una bambolina.

Fra Felix, amidst another cloud of incense, reenters the hatch, laden with bicycles. The sky, with the sun, moon, and stars, moves gently like scenery.

7 h. 50–11 h. 50

Hora baixa, els becs de gas escampen damunt el meu carrer una tendra claror d'apotecari. El barber penja sota la barba postissa d'una carota de gegant el vell globus polsós de porcellana, i l'encén.

L'ombra del campanar tomba agònica damunt el passeig, i un número 12 fosforescent la tatua recorrent els seus membres convulsos. Pengim-penjam, a totes les acàcies ballen, indescriptiblement tronades, centenars de parells de sabates.

Mal cobrint-se les nueses amb un tros de primer full de *La Vanguardia*, surten de llurs palaus, pelosos, els Sàtirs. Un monster mitològic, caval-cant el seu cavall alat, branda, al cim de Sant Pere Màrtir, un manyoc de números esgroguëits de *El Mundo Ilustrado* (1.a època) i il·lumina els flancs de la muntanya. Quan s'acaba de fer nit, amb el seu buf poderós fa oscil·lar suaument les constel·lacions.

7:50–11:50

In the evening, the gas lamps spread an apothecary's soft light over my street. The barber hangs an old, dusty porcelain globe under the false beard on a *gegant*'s droll face. And then he illuminates it.

The shadow of the bell tower turns agonized over the boulevard, and a phosphorescent number 12 tattoos it along its convulsive members. Hundreds of paired shoes, indescribably shabby, dance higgledy-piggledy with all the acacias.

The shaggy Satyrs emerge from their palaces, scarcely covering their nakedness with scraps from the front pages of *La Vanguardia*. At the top of Sant Pere Màrtir, a mythological monster, astride his wingèd steed, brandishes a handful of yellowed issues of *El Mundo Ilustrado* (1st series) and lights up the flanks of the mountain. When night falls, his powerful bluster sends the constellations gently swaying.

Plaça Catalunya—Pedralbes

Acabava de llençar el meu bitllet, quan l'inspector, bufat, em refusà l'excusa: calia abonar de nou el trajecte. Contra el costum, fou ell mateix qui em lliurà rebut: un manyoc de bitllets multicolor em floria de sobte entre mans mentre l'inspector em befava amb cadència perquè distingís el meu. El seu esguard, voraç, em xuclava les rels del cabell i em sentia per moments esdevenir calb. Hauria alçat el braç, amenaçador, si la sensació de tenir-lo amputat sota l'aixella no m'hagués aturat la voluntat i enterbolit el seny, el qual s'obstinava a engrandir una llàntia groga que l'inspector lluïa arran mateix d'un botó amb imatgeria d'ex-vot.

El vehicle, un tram d'imperial, era, en aquells moments, sense passatgers; jo, que el sabia tot ocupat, en vaig ésser sorprès: podia jurar que no havíem fet cap parada. Em va venir una angoixa que m'anegà del tot en adonar-me que mancava el conductor i que el trajecte que recorríem m'era desconegut. Només tres xiprers de prop de l'estació de Gràcia foren copsats de llisquentes, però desplaçats del tot.

Tot d'una, l'inspector canvià el seu esguard obsessionant en tendresa complaent. Li ho anava a agrair quan em sorprengué la seva figura: duia barba i jo podia assegurar que la seva cara era rasa en aparèixer-se'm. M'aconhortà el veure que duia rellotge-braçalet i uns botins la color dels quals ni escolant la memòria entre celles no puc precisar. Parà el vehicle i l'esma em va empènyer a baixar. Vaig intentar de fer-ho primer, quan l'inspector m'alliçonà tot polsant un piu automàtic que abaixà l'estrep a una profunditat que impossibilitava el salt.

Allunyats de la parada, vaig mirar enrere i em vaig adonar que en aquell paratge no hi havia instal·lació tramviària. El tram, sense rodes, amb la

Plaça Catalunya—Pedralbes

I had just thrown away my ticket when the inspector, full of self-importance, refused my excuse: I would have to pay for the journey again. Contrary to the usual practice, he himself gave me a receipt. A bunch of multicolored tickets suddenly bloomed in his hands as he demanded derisively that I pick out mine. His voracious stare sucked the roots from my scalp, and I soon felt I was growing bald. I would have raised my arm menacingly if the lugubrious feeling of getting it amputated at the armpit hadn't sapped my will and clouded my judgment. I persisted in exaggerating a yellow lamp that the inspector was shining right next to a button with ex-voto imagery.

The vehicle, a double-decker tram, was without any passengers at that moment. I was surprised: I felt sure it was completely filled. I could have sworn we hadn't made any stops. I was flooded with anxiety when I noticed the driver was missing and the route we were traveling was unfamiliar. I caught only three cypresses close to the Gràcia station, slipping by, but they were completely displaced.

All of a sudden the inspector changed his haunting stare into obliging tenderness. I was on the verge of thanking him when his figure surprised me: he was wearing a beard, and I could have sworn his face had been shaven when he appeared before me. I was consoled to see that he was wearing a wristwatch and spats, whose color drained from my memory so I couldn't be precise about them. The vehicle stopped, and instinct drove me to get off. At first I tried to do it on my own, but the inspector showed me how. He pressed an automatic pin which lowered the footboard to a depth that made the leap impossible.

As the stop receded, I looked behind and noticed that no tram cable had been installed. The tram, minus wheels, its coachwork smashed and

carrosseria esbotzada i el tròlei malmès, tenia l'aspecte de fer anyades a desdir que es podria sobre l'areny a l'embat del temps.

Arribats al peu d'una alzina, l'inspector va reprendre aquell mirar que impossibilitava un refús i m'obligà a cenyir, damunt la carn viva, un cilici. Vaig creure en el meu pròxim traspàs. Enmig del turment vaig endevinar que les pues, cares als penitents, havien estat substituïdes hàbilment per lletres d'acer reblat del caràcter de les que en els catàlegs de fundició tipogràfica hom anomena *titulars grotesques*, i llegia, closos els ulls, però a través de ferides sagnants, un poema de Ramon Rucabado.

M'anegà una rara suor com si als meus anys m'obliguessin davant la vida escarlata a una actitud a la Remy de Gourmont. La bromera que em donava el martiri esdevingué depilatori eficaç i esquitxà la faç del meu botxí xollant-lo del tot. Em trobava davant per davant del poeta López-Picó, el qual, esglaiat d'haver estat descobert en el seu crim, submergí el braç en un grop de fosca que s'escorria entorn nostre, emmascarant-se'n la mà per a embrutar-se'n la cara i disfressar-la.

El vaig mirar de fit a fit i restà èrtic. Amb l'ull esquerre projectava damunt meu una fredor que em glaçava els ossos fins a polvoritzar-los; l'ull dret es féu escorredís de gairell i, desprenent-se de l'òrbita, s'allunyà per l'horitzó i espià per ciutat si el poeta Folguera havia estat testimoni de la meva tortura. Confiat que el crim romania secret, l'ull miraculós, magnificat per les esplendors del Pecat Secret, aparegué altre cop a la vista. Hesità entre les branques d'un roure esponerós i s'enfilà amb un llampegueig a cada moment més viu vers el firmament estelat.

El poeta havia desaparegut del meu davant; una lleu letícia m'enduia el cor mentre el cilici es desprenia del cos. L'ull de l'ex-inspector era un estel més d'un guspireig insòlit, que destil·lava una mel que m'amorosia els llavis i que, en socarrimar el fil de la meva memòria, em divinitzava tot entonant, en acció de gràcies, els càntics més bells de Schahrazada.

its poles broken, looked as if it had spent too many years rotting in sand, beaten by weather.

On arriving at the foot of an oak, the inspector put on that stare again, barring any rebuff and forcing me to don a hair shirt against my bare flesh. I believed my death was near. Amid my torment, I guessed that thorns, so dear to penitents, had been cleverly replaced by riveted steel letters in the font that type foundry catalogues call "Headline Grotesque." My eyes closed, I read a poem by Ramon Rucabado through bloody wounds.

A strange sweat drenched me as if at my age I were forced to assume an attitude before the scarlet life à la Remy de Gourmont. The foamy saliva bestowed by my martyrdom became an effective depilatory, and splattering my tormentor's face, it sheared him clean. I found myself facing the poet Josep Maria López-Picó, who, appalled at being discovered in his crime, immersed his arm in the dark cloud that oozed around us, blackening his hand to soil his face and disguise it.

I looked him up and down and remained rigid. His left eye projected over mine a coldness that froze me to the point of pulverizing my bones; his right eye had slid sideways, and working itself loose from the socket, it moved toward the horizon, spying on the city to learn whether the poet Joaquim Folguera had witnessed my torture. Confident that the crime remained secret, the miraculous eye, magnified by the splendor of the Hidden Sin, came into view once again. It hesitated among the branches of a luxuriant oak and climbed toward the starry firmament with a flash of lightning that grew ever brighter.

The poet had disappeared in front of me. A hint of gaiety brought round my heart while the hair shirt loosened itself from my body. The ex-inspector's eye was another star of an unwonted glitter. It distilled a honey that softened my lips and, in singeing the thread of my memory, exalted me to the heavens while intoning the most charming canticles of Scheherazade in a gesture of gratitude.

Pepa, la lletera

Pepa, la lletera, té les cames més fines del món. Fa vuit dies, al ball del carrer de Sant Vicenç, totes les noies li ho deien. Va anar a dormir tan a deshora, que son germà, matiner, ja apariava la bicicleta. Quan dues hores més tard pujava Clos amunt, a cada mà dos pots de llet enormes, els ulls se li aclucaven. Veia, ballant, deu mil parelles amb un clavell de llustrina al front; dels fanals japonesos esberlats, els flams s'escapaven cap al cel i l'omplien d'estels incomptables. Les cases de banda i banda havien desaparegut. I, tot d'una, els dansaires. Pepa es veia sola al món, de cara al cel lluminós. En entreobrir els ulls, era davant el convent de les monges. Sor Roser la renyà: era tan tard! Deixà els pots al graó i, entre reny i reny, els ulls se li tornaren a cloure. Aleshores, tots els balcons i totes les finestres del Clos s'esbatanaren, se sentí un batec d'ales dolcíssim, i de cada obertura en sortí un àngel. S'acostaven silenciosament i ordenadament a Pepa, i omplien llurs petits gerros argentats. En descloure els ulls, els pots de llet eren buits i el carrer era ple d'un perfum de roses.

El diumenge següent, en sortint, a les tres de la matinada, del ball de La Violeta, li vaig dir:—Pepa! Quina son aquest matí. Em va respondre que els dilluns santa Eulàlia li feia la feina.

Pepa the Milkmaid

Pepa the milkmaid has the finest legs in the world. Eight days ago, at the ball in Carrer de Sant Vicenç, all the girls were saying so. She went to sleep so late that, in the morning, her brother was already getting his bicycle in order. When she climbed up Clos de Sant Francesc two hours later, two enormous cans of milk in each hand, her eyes were closing. She saw ten thousand couples dancing with satin carnations in their hair. The flames from the torn Japanese lanterns escaped toward the sky, filling it with countless stars. The houses on either side had disappeared. And so, all of a sudden, had the dancers. Pepa saw herself alone in the world, facing the luminous sky. She was standing before the nuns' convent, her eyes half open. Sister Roser scolded her: she was so late! She set the cans on the step and, amid the scolding, her eyes were closing again. At that moment, all the balconies and windows of Clos de Sant Francesc were opened wide. She heard the gentlest beating of wings, and an angel emerged from every opening. They drew near Pepa, quietly and in an orderly way, and they filled their little silver pitchers. When she opened her eyes, the milk cans were empty, and the street was suffused with the scent of roses.

The following Sunday, as we were leaving the ball at La Violeta at three, I said to her: "Pepa! You'll sleep late this morning." She responded that on Mondays Santa Eulàlia does the work for her.

Sense simbolisme

El director de la banda municipal és tan corpulent que ocupa mitja plaça. Quan estén el braç tots els nois del poble allarguen les mans per fer-hi tombarelles com a la barra fixa. Però criden molt i el director s'enfada. El director és un home singular: creu que la gent hi acut per la seva orquestra i que el poble aplaudeix els grans autors. Aleshores s'irrita per qualsevol soroll, i els algutzirs fan callar els ocells i tanquen les fonts. Però la música de banda, en el silenci, és impura. Els grans músics encara no s'han adonat que llurs composicions són per a acompanyar només, discretament, el brogit inharmònic del veïnat aplegat a la festa. Sense cavallets, enamorats, sac de gemecs i piules, què seria, oh grans mestres, la vostra obra?

Un dia vam pintar un teló de fons que representava una casa amb dues finestres ovalades i la vam penjar a la plaça de manera que se'n menjava una quarta part. Ens hi vam amagar al darrere tot de nois i noies. A mitja simfonia de Haendel el teló, al mateix moment que jo pessigava l'anca de Gertrudis, va caure i vam restar en descobert. Gertrudis va fer un xiscle enjogassat. La banda va parar en sec. Mai cap compositor no ha escrit ni escriurà una nota equivalent al crit de Gertrudis llançat, a mitjanit, a plaça oberta.

El director, convertit en un Ogre de Gustau Doré, ens empaità terriblement amenaçador, carrer avall. Com dues ales verdes se'ns obriren misteriosament les portes de casa la cotillaire i ens refugiàrem darrere l'espectre sedós d'un maniquí.

En desvetllar-nos teníem entre mans, desinflat i a trossos, un esfèric de paper amb la vera efígie del director de la banda.

Without Symbolism

The conductor of the municipal band is so corpulent that he takes up half the square. When he extends an arm, all the village children stretch out their hands to turn somersaults as if they were on the horizontal bar. But they shout quite a lot, and the conductor gets cross. He is a singular man: he believes that people come for his orchestra and the town applauds the great composers. Thus he flies into a temper at the slightest noise, and the constables hush up the birds and shut off the fountains. But in the silence the band's music is impure. The illustrious musicians have still not realized that their compositions are nothing more than the discreet accompaniment to the inharmonious din of the neighbors gathered at the festival. Without carousels, lovers, bagpipes, and firecrackers, what would your work be, revered masters?

One day we painted a backdrop that represented a house with two oval windows, and we hung it in the square so that it consumed a quarter of the space. We hid all the boys and girls behind it. Midway through a symphony by Handel, just at the moment when I pinched Gertrudis's bottom, the backdrop fell, and we were caught in the act. Gertrudis let out a frisky squeal. The band stopped dead. Never has any composer penned a note (nor will any) equivalent to the cry that Gertrudis uttered in the open square at midnight.

The conductor, converted into an ogre from Gustave Doré, chased after us down the street, terribly menacing. Like two green wings, the doors of the corset maker's house mysteriously opened for us, and we sought refuge behind the silken specter of a mannequin.

When we awoke, our hands held a paper sphere with the spitting image of the conductor, deflated and in tatters.

Notes sobre la mar

1

La sorpresa fou quan en haver pogut retirar, després de molts d'esforços, els bastidors on hi havia pintats tot d'atributs marítims, descobrírem la cleda misteriosa dels cavalls negres que, en ésser nit, vaguen a milers i milers per la platja amb una estrella al front.

Notes on the Sea

1

The surprise occurred when, after spending much effort to remove the scenery where various maritime motifs had been painted, we discovered the mysterious corral of the black horses. Come nightfall, they wander the beach by the thousands, a star on their foreheads.

2

Ben lligat el nas de cartó, grotesc, em passejava pel moll amb un imponent diccionari de sinònims sota el braç. El barquer, vulgues no vulgues, em féu navegar mar endins. Era un pastor anglicà, i em volia demostrar com els miracles més bells s'han esdevingut a la mar. En adonar-se, però, del meu nas arbitrari, tingué la polidesa de calar-se el seu. Aleshores, emfàtic, em digué que només la vanitat dels homes fa que, en el viure humà, del nostre planeta en diguin la Terra, però que Déu i els sants en diuen, en llur llenguatge etern, la Mar; que la terra era només en el nostre planeta un accident, un fenomen transitori. "Els homes—em deia—són la colomassa de la mar." La gran inconeguda dels homes era, per al meu barquer, una peixera esfèrica errant pels espais celestes per a esbargiment dels àngels.

2

Wearing a grotesque pasteboard nose, firmly fastened, I was strolling along the quay with an imposing dictionary of synonyms beneath my arm. The boatman had me sail far out to sea, whether or not I fancied it. He was an Anglican priest, and he wanted to show me how the most beautiful miracles happened on the watery main. Upon noticing my arbitrary nose, however, he had the elegance to don his. Then he told me, emphatically, that only the vanity of men causes them to call our planet Earth, in the human scheme of things, whereas God and the saints call it Sea in their eternal parlance, and the earth on our planet was only an accident, a transitory phenomenon. "Men," he told me, "are the pigeon excrement of the sea." For my boatman, the great unknown among men was a spherical fish bowl wandering through celestial space for the diversion of the angels.

3

La mar, aquell matí, era un sòlid rectangular incolor i transparent com el cristall. Damunt seu, projectant-se oblíquament en llargues, immensurables ombres còniques i cilíndriques, s'hi sostenien rares i originals figures de cel·luloide. Els pescadors, refets de llur sorpresa, asseguraven que eren l'esquelet dels estels, expel·lits del fons de la mar en produir-se aquell fenomen.

3

The sea, that morning, was a solid rectangle, colorless and transparent as crystal. On its surface stood celluloid figures, strange and sui generis, projecting themselves obliquely in long, immeasurable shadows shaped like cones and cylinders. The fishermen, after recovering from their surprise, affirmed that they were the skeletons of stars, expelled from the depths of the sea when that phenomenon was produced.

4

De levita i copalta negre, enguantats de negre també, els tres cavallers gesticulaven còmicament davant la mar color de taronja. En topar-me, recularen admirats. Sorprès jo a la vegada, vaig preguntar-os amb emoció precipitada: —Vosaltres també per ací? I riguérem follament. Aleshores vaig córrer a posar-me el vestit negre, el copalta, els guants i a dibuixar-me amb carbó tres amples arrugues al front. Riba enllà, riba enllà, recordàvem, amb gests teatrals i simètrics, l'altra mar taronja on un dia imprecisable ens havíem topat també tots quatre, idènticament abillats, i en el qual, riba enllà, riba enllà, també a grans riallades, intentàvem de recordar a quin segle, davant el país de la mar taronja, havíem discutit una vegada tots quatre a quin planeta pertanyia la mar on una vegada ells tres i jo, tots de negre, i rient, ens esforçàvem a recordar . . .

4

Wearing black frock coats and top hats, as well as black gloves, the three horsemen gesticulated comically before the orange-colored sea. When they bumped into me, they recoiled in admiration. Immediately taken by surprise, I asked them with precipitate emotion: "Are you here as well?" And we burst into mad laughter. Then I dashed off to throw on a black coat, top hat, and gloves, and with coal I drew three wide wrinkles on my forehead. On the far shore, way over on the far shore, we remembered, with gestures that were at once theatrical and symmetric, the other orange sea where on an unspecifiable day all four of us also bumped into each other, dressed identically, way over on the far shore, on the far shore, likewise with raucous laughter, we endeavored to remember, standing before the country with the orange sea, which century it was when all four of us once discussed which planet contains the sea where the three of you and I, all in black, and laughing, once strained to remember . . .

5

En acabar-se el ball, el cel i la mar són una sola tenebra. El darrer estel naufraga en un escull paorós i a la línia de l'horitzó, de l'arabesc de les enormes madrèpores, monstruoses, en resta una vaga fosforescència. Només entre la mar i el cel, solitàries, les mitges vermelles de Gertrudis pengen, com un parrac de bandera mil·lenària, de l'arbre d'un vaixell serpent d'Oscher, el víking famós.

5

As the ball comes to an end, sky and sea form a single darkness. The last star founders on a frightening reef, and at the line of the horizon a vague phosphorescence lingers from the arabesque of stony coral, so monstrously enormous. Between sea and sky lies nothing but Gertrudis's red stockings, hanging solitary, like a scrap of an ancient flag, from the mast of a serpent ship commanded by Oscher, the famous Viking.

6

De lluny tothom crida: la mar! la mar!; però en ésser-hi al davant, calla hores i hores. Avui, una multitud d'homes i de dones, nus com la mateixa mar, la desafiava a riallades. Creien que llur pell bruna seria per a la mar un afrodisíac desvetllador de la seva doble passió hermafrodita. Però la mar, púdica, s'ha recollit sota un auri mantell on les ombres captives de la multitud teixien, amb vagues imatges vanament obscenes, un irregular serrell.

6

From afar everyone shouts: The sea! The sea! But when they stand before it, they are hushed for hours on end. Today, a multitude of men and women, naked as the sea itself, were defying it with boisterous laughter. They thought their brown skin would prove to be an aphrodisiac to the sea, arousing its double, hermaphroditic passion. But the sea modestly withdrew beneath its golden mantle where the captive shadows of the multitude weave, with vague, vainly obscene images, an irregular fringe.

Notes del *Diari*

No són cases; no és el meu carrer. Sota una xarxa de cordes inútils, sento el brogit de la mar que no veuré mai més. Faig un esforç mortal i arribo a entendre els mots gruixuts que al fons d'un túnel sense fi es diuen un home amb brusa de pintor i N'Alexandre Plana vençut sota el pes de les arracades A. B. que li pengen de les orelles. Damunt la pell de paquiderm que cobreix el cel, per sempre hi ha pintats cavalls negres i pneumàtics amb llur funda.

Notes from the *Daybook*

They are not houses; it is not my street. Beneath a net of useless rope, I hear the roar of the sea where I shall never again set my eyes. I make a mortal effort and come to understand the dense words spoken in the depths of an endless tunnel by a man in a painter's smock and Alexandre Plana, who is overwehelmed by the weight of the earrings with the initials A. B. hanging from his ears. On the pachyderm skin that covers the sky, black horses are painted indelibly along with tires and their hubcaps.

Perquè m'he pintat la faç de negre, la fornera, amb un quinqué a la mà, em mira gelosa. Però sé que ignora les pràctiques libidinoses del tintorer i que ara faran un sostre a banda i banda dels carrers que no deixarà veure més les estrelles. Les parets de la tintoreria són peludes i, a mitja nit, si les palpeu bé, hi trobareu amagats ulls de noies adolescents. Els de l'aprenenta, que eren blaus com la combinació que va estrenar la Dolors pel seu sant, els tinc jo. Quan dormo me'ls poso damunt el ventre.

Because I painted my face black, the baker, an oil lamp in her hand, eyes me with jealousy. But I know that she is unaware of the dyer's libidinous practices and the plan afoot to build a roof over the streets which will forevermore block the stars from sight. The walls of the dyeworks are hairy, and at midnight, if you touch them carefully, you will find the eyes of adolescent girls hidden there. The apprentice's eyes, which were as blue as the slip that Dolors first wore on her saint's day—I have them in my possession. When I sleep, I lay them on my belly.

Hi ha cavalls per portals i finestres. Hi ha enagos vermelles al cap del carrer que tapen la nuesa de Gertrudis. Darrera Gertrudis hi ha el mar i damunt el mar sura la perruca que penjava del portal de la Vaqueria. El perruquer, sota el dosser argentat que dóna entrada a la llòbrega botiga, somriu sarcàstic. La seva dona, amb un bigoti postís, que li penja més del costat dret, desempolsa les testes decapitades de les seves tres filles. L'anell que porto a la mà dreta pertany a la segona. En forma de segell conté, dibuixant una E (es deia Elvira), el seu cordó umbilical.

There are horses by doors and windows. There are red petticoats at the head of the street to hide Gertrudis's nakedness. Behind Gertrudis is the sea, and on the sea floats the wig that used to hang from the door of the dairy. The wig maker, beneath the silver canopy at the entrance of his gloomy shop, smiles sarcastically. His wife, who wears a false moustache that droops lower on the right side, dusts the severed heads of their three daughters. The ring I wear on my right hand belongs to the second. It contains, in the form of a seal, her umbilical cord, which traces an E (she was called Elvira).

Ombres darrere els lilàs

Mil ales rosa cobrien el cel. Portes i finestres eren closes, i de cantonada a cantonada voleiaven banderes i gallardets. L'ombra oval es desvià carrer amunt amb majestat aterridora. L'endemà, les imatges dels sants de la parròquia aparegueren decapitades.

Shadows behind Lilacs

A thousand pink wings covered the sky. Doors and windows were closed, and from one street corner to the next flags and pennants were flying. An oval shadow was deflected up the street with terrifying majesty. The next day, the saints' images in the parish church appeared to be decapitated.

Fou diumenge passat, a les tres de la tarda, sobre el pont del passeig, que un embriac occí una dona per amor d'una rosa que l'homicida abandonà damunt el toll de sang. Ja el diumenge abans hom havia assenyalat un fet idèntic al mateix indret i a la mateixa hora. Pressento per a avui un crim equivalent. Em cal, doncs, advertir el taverner i avisar la policia. Però, Déu meu, i si fos jo l'assassí? Vet ací el meu got vessant de vi, el carmí dels teus llavis, del teu si, del teu sexe, reflectit dins la tèrbola beguda roja. Aboqueu més vi, Rafel!, són dos quarts de tres; al pont del passeig hi ha una dona amb una rosa a la mà i el meu coltell és fi com l'aresta d'un estel.

Last Sunday, at three in the afternoon, on the bridge over the boulevard, a drunken man killed a woman for the love of a rose which the murderer abandoned in the pool of blood. The previous Sunday, in fact, someone had noted that an identical act would occur at the same place and the same time. I have the foreboding that an equivalent crime will be committed today. I must therefore warn the owner of the taverna and notify the police. But, my God, what if I am the assassin? Here before me stands a glass brimming with wine, the carmine of your lips, your nipples, your sex, reflected in the turbid red drink. Pour out my wine, Rafael! It is half past two. On the bridge over the boulevard stands a woman with a rose in her hand, and my knife is as sharp as the edge of a star.

El Díaz i el Vicente s'han deixat embargar el piano de maneta. Quina tristesa d'avui endavant, les tardes de diumenge! Ombres absurdes vagaran indecises pels caps de carrer i l'idiota de la taverna es passarà la tarda abocant oli des de la finestra. Els lilàs cenyiran els murs, s'estendran per les cornises i teixiran de cantonada a cantonada espesses cortines impenetrables. A les cases del passatge ja no hi viurà mai més ningú, i les danses que hi ballaran a entrada de fosc seran, als meus ulls, invisibles. Només percebré l'àgil trepig dels peus minyons damunt l'asfalt i, en ésser nit, els estels que entre mil flonjors blau-negre simularan trèmules mamelles adolescents.

Díaz and Vicente have allowed the player piano to be impounded. What melancholy from this day forward! The Sunday afternoons! Absurd shadows will wander indecisive down the street, and the idiot from the taverna will spend the afternoon pouring oil from the window. The lilacs will cling to the walls, spread over the cornices, and weave dense, impenetrable curtains from corner to corner. No one will ever live again in the houses on the passageway, and the dances that are danced there at dusk will be invisible to my eyes. I shall perceive only the agile tread of youthful feet on the asphalt and, at nightfall, the stars that simulate quivering adolescent breasts amid the expanse of blue-black sponginess.

Nois i noies del meu poble, que malcobreixen llur groga nuditat sota gases de tendres colors subtils, juguen cada capvespre a la plaça. Llur veu hi ressona com en un celler, i els ocells s'hi acosten per escandallar amb llur bec els blavosos estanys de llurs ulls. L'altre dia, tot estrafent la veu amb un megàfon, vaig intentar de barrejar-me en llur joc; però, nois, noies i ocells, eren ombres entre ombres. Davant meu, entre la plaça deserta i el cel, s'elevava, tràgicament delator, un filferro en espiral.

Boys and girls from my village, who badly cover their yellow nakedness with gauze of subtle, tender colors, play in the square every evening. Their voices resonate as in a cellar, and the birds' beaks draw near to sound the depths of the blue pools in their eyes. The other day, mimicking their voices with a megaphone, I attempted to join their game. But boys, girls, and birds were shadows among shadows. Before me, a spiral wire—tragic informer—rose between the deserted square and the sky.

Perquè l'home que ven fruits secs sota els porxos de la plaça s'ha posat un casquet turc, vermell, homes i infants del meu poble han adoptat el cobrecaps exòtic, i dones i donzelles han ornat llurs cabells amb roselles enceses. Del matí al vespre, la marea roja submergeix els vells carrerons, fins ara reialme dels fantasmes, i s'estén pel raval, on sojorna el ferrer de les dues testes. Tots dos, el senyor rector i jo, hem resistit el corrent tirànic. Per defugir-lo, el senyor rector, amagant-se sota el seu ample mantell negre, ha pres figura de gàrgola centenària a la cornisa del campanar; i jo, convertit en l'orat del poble, em passo el dia dibuixant la imatge del sol per les parets i els seus atributs divins.

Because the dried-fruit vendor beneath the arcade in the square wore a Turkish skullcap, in red, men and children from my village adopted the exotic close-fitting cap, while women and girls adorned their hair with fiery poppies. From morning to evening, the red tide submerges the old alleyways, till now the realm of ghosts, and it reaches as far as the outskirts, where the two-headed blacksmith sojourns. Both the parish priest and I have resisted the tyrannical fashion. To avoid it, the priest, concealing himself beneath his ample black cloak, has taken the shape of the century-old gargoyle on the cornice of the bell tower. I, in turn, transformed into the village idiot, spend the day drawing on walls the image of the sun, as well as its divine attributes.

Ni els peixos en semicercle no eren adés ocells ni són ara figuracions octogonals. Llurs giravolts entorn dels tres botons de laca vermella que floten en aquesta nit tan obscura, no es confondran mai amb els arabescs que dibuixen els rulls de la grossa nina que has amagat impunement sota el sofà.

The fish swimming in a semicircle were not birds just a moment ago, nor are they now octagonal figurations. Their revolutions around the three red lacquer buttons floating in this night so dark will never be confused with the arabesques that sketch the curls of the large doll you have hidden beneath the sofa with impunity.

Feixos d'heura davant de cada casa. Tan de matí, tot fumant la vostra pipa, heu fet, mon Ton, bella esporgada! Fa molta de fresca aquesta matinada, i els carrers són, en aquesta hora, ben solitaris. A totes les entrades hi ha una creu de palma, i darrere les portes dels cancells i per les cantonades hom sent el xiuxiueig dels àngels que omplen la vila en néixer el dia, i s'hi conten entre ells llurs rondalles. No feu brogit, Ton! Aturem les nostres passes. Els àngels, com els ratolins, callen en sentir el trepig més bla i fugen tot deixant un rastre de filagarses rosa. No feu tant de brogit, Ton!

El carrer és més solitari que mai. Fa molt de fred aquesta matinada. No fou ahir tarda, darrere un paravent d'heura, que em digueres que Ton, el vostre jardiner, l'havíeu enterrat el dia abans?

Bundles of ivy before every house. You've done a splendid job of pruning, my Ton, so early in the morning, and all the while smoking your pipe! The dawn air is very fresh, and at this hour the streets are virtually deserted. At every entrance appears a cross made of palm, and behind the outer doors as well as on street corners the angels' murmuring is heard filling the village at daybreak. They are telling tales among themselves. Don't raise a racket, Ton! Let's stop in our tracks. Angels, like mice, fall silent when they hear the softest tread, and they flee, leaving a trail of pink raveled threads. Don't raise such a racket, Ton!

The street is more deserted than ever. The dawn air is very cold. Wasn't it yesterday afternoon, behind an ivy trellis, that you told me your gardener Ton had been buried the day before?

Palplantat a la porta i de cara al carrer, aquest homenàs no em deixa passar. L'amplada de la seva espatlla em tapa mig carrer i roman amb la testa i els braços estirats.—Faré tard a l'Institut; em cal examinar!—Faré tard a l'oficina!—M'esperen a casa . . . !—. Em poso a plorar. És inútil. Tot d'éssers d'ales negres aixequen entre l'espatlla d'aquest homenàs i el cel una pantalla flonja, on s'ofeguen, en ésser nit, els estels. Si l'homenàs tingués peus, m'hi deixaria caure; però tot ell és un cos quadrat i massís, contra el qual no puc lluitar. El cartó-pasta de la seva testa regalima encara vernís i el seu bigoti roig és pintat de fresc.—Et conec, maniquí; restaré sempre més sota la teva guarda. Cada vespre, quan tanco els ulls per a adormir-me, per l'obertura de l'angle que dibuixen el teu coll i la teva espatlla dreta les verges passen en caravana enmig d'un silenci rosa; o, damunt un paisatge de contorns irisats, s'obren els estanys sense nom, al fons dels quals les astèries, les ofiüres, les madrèpores i les anèmones són vidres cristal·lins per on circulen les perles que estotgen les gotes de sang que nodreixen la meva zoantropia.

Stock-still at the door, facing the street, this hulk doesn't let me pass. The broadness of his shoulders blocks me midway, and he remains with head erect and arms extended. "You're making me late for the Institute; I have to give an examination!" "You're making me late for the office!" "They're expecting me at home!" . . . I burst into tears. It is useless. Between this man's shoulders and the sky, a multitude of black-winged creatures raises a spongy screen where, since night has fallen, the stars drown. If the hulk had feet, I would fall at them. But he is only a square, massive body, against which I can't fight. The papier-mâché of his head still drips varnish, and his red moustache is freshly painted. "I know about you, mannequin. I shall forever remain in your custody. Every night, when I close my eyes to sleep, through the opening of the angle sketched by your neck and your right shoulder, the maidens pass in a group amid pink silence. Or name-less lakes open over a landscape of iridescent contours, and in their depths star-stones, starfish, coral, and anemones are crystalline glass through which pearls flow, encasing the drops of blood that feed my zoanthropy."

Destenyits per la pluja, amagats tota la tarda en un estret passadís entre bocois, els nois del meu carrer ens avinguérem a esperar que es fes del tot fosc per a posar-nos els vestits morats i plantar al mig de la plaça un embut enorme, d'un diàmetre idèntic al perímetre d'aquella i tan alt com la torre de can Pomeret. En haver-se apagat el darrer llum del poble, pintàrem de negre les cases de la plaça i penjàrem entre terrat i terrat unes bambolines que figuraven uns núvols grisos o una columna de fum de locomotora en dia bromós. Quan era tot llest, ens amagàrem sota les voltes de la farmàcia per espiar de quina manera la lluna es deixaria atreure per aquell parany enginyós d'alumini. Però en ésser les dotze, s'obriren, amb gran terrabastall, les portes de la fleca, en sortí una dona carregada la testa amb sis pans en columna, i es perdé l'encís d'aquella nit.

Faded by the rain, hidden for the entire afternoon among barrels in a narrow alleyway, we boys from my street agreed to wait till darkness descended to put on our purple suits and set an enormous funnel in the middle of the square, identical in diameter to the square itself and as tall as the tower of Can Pomeret. After the last light in the village had gone out, we painted the houses in the square black, and between the roofs we hung backdrops that represented a few gray clouds or a column of smoke from a locomotive on a misty day. When everything was ready, we hid beneath the arches of the pharmacy to spy on how the moon would let herself be attracted by that ingenious aluminum snare. But when midnight arrived, the doors of the bakery opened with a tremendous din, a woman came out carrying six loaves stacked on her head, and the spell of that night was broken.

Tot just m'acabava d'obrir ell mateix la porta de casa seva, el meu amic m'acostà a una pissarra que agafava tot un pany de paret. Sense dir res, hi escriví, amb difícil cal·ligrafia, *stop*. Amb prou feines si jo l'havia reconegut: la seva famosa corpulència, que mai no em deixa veure prou bé la mar, s'havia esvanit fins al punt de transfigurar-se en l'efígie d'un singular amic absent. Jo provava de sil·labejar la consigna: *stop*. La impotència més restrictiva m'ofegava el mot a flor de llavi. També en ell el mateix mot pugnava, infortunat, per materialitzar-se, però, féu un esforç que em caldrà agrair-li sempre més, i pogué arribar a alçar el braç esquerre per a assenyalar-me la finestra. Vaig comprendre l'abast de la vera amistat: totes les carreteres que s'hi albiraven s'havien doblegat i es precipitaven, verticals, en un fall pregon. Una veu exclamà, alta per damunt les nostres testes:—És la més bella vitrina de pneumàtics que he vist en ma vida. I una altra veu més alta encara:—Les trompes dels orifanys no cediran mai a cap de les temptacions de la vida moderna.

No sooner had my friend himself greeted me at the door of his home than he led me to a blackboard which covered a stretch of wall. Without speaking, he wrote the English word *stop* on it in difficult handwriting. I had hardly recognized him: his legendary corpulence, which had never allowed me a clear enough glimpse of the sea, had so wasted away as to transfigure him into the effigy of a singularly absent friend. I tried to syllabify the order: *stop*. The most restrictive impotence smothered the word at my lips. In him too the word haplessly struggled to materialize. Yet he made an effort which obliged me to be forever grateful to him, going so far as to raise his right arm to point at the window. I understood the reach of true friendship: every road we could spot had curved and was now rushing headlong toward a sheer cliff. A voice cried out, loud, over our heads: "It's the most lovely tire display I've ever seen in my life." Then another voice, louder still: "The trunks of oliphaunts shall never yield to the temptations of modernity."

Retorn a la natura

Per un filferro llançat per damunt el més absurd dels abismes, llisca, com perla de rosada, l'espectre dels teus guants.

Return to Nature

Along a wire suspended over the most absurd abyss slips, like a pearl of dew, the specter of your gloves.

Fugir, fugir . . . Però l'ombra dels avets recull l'ombra dels ocells malèfics i al fons de l'horitzó mil ales blaves han abatut llur vol. Fugir . . . Hi ha una mà a cada estança, hi ha uns llavis al llindar de les cabanes, hi ha uns braços darrera els troncs caiguts. Hi ha un cel tan baix que no em deixa passar. Fugir, fugir . . . Cèrcols de joc, cèrcols de glaç i els meus peus amputats damunt les catifes inútils del Gran Castell.

Flee, flee . . . The shadow of fir trees gathers the shadow of malign birds, and at the edge of the horizon a thousand blue wings have ceased their flight. Flee . . . A hand appears at every standstill, lips at the lintel of every cottage, arms behind every fallen trunk. A sky so low that it blocks my path. Flee, flee . . . Hoops in play, hoops of ice, and my severed feet on the useless carpets of the Gran Castell.

L'últim ocell es desprèn de la seva ombra com d'una disfressa damunt el macadam inútil. Qui abandona entre les meves mans aquest guant perfumat?

The last bird shakes off its shadow like a disguise on the pointless macadam. Who abandons this perfumed glove in my hands?

Cap mà no em diu adéu; però per les cantonades i al fons de tot del carrer, mil mans amputades, en aquest capvespre morat, suren, cauen o s'allunyen amb lentitud vegetal.

No hand bids me farewell. But at the corners and the very end of the street, in this purple dusk, a thousand severed hands float, fall, or withdraw with vegetal slowness.

Per les obertures tubulars davallen grosses àmfores esmaltades. Del fons de les cisternes unes veus desordenades em criden pel meu nom. Però si em mogués del capdavall del soterrani, la meva testa—aranya marmòria coronada de tentacles cristal·lins—llanguiria sota les lluors quitranoses del dia. Quina vida ardent s'escorre per les venes robustes que palpiten al llarg de les parets del passadís . . . !

Huge enameled amphoras descend from tubular openings. From the bottom of cisterns chaotic voices call me by name. But if I left the back of the cellar, my head—marble spider crowned with crystalline tentacles—would languish beneath the tarry radiance of the day. What blazing life drains from the robust veins pulsing along the walls of the passageway!

Só jo que porto, més alt que tots, l'ocellàs d'alumini que posem, a les nits de lluna, damunt la font de la pedrera. Pere, Lluís! On sou? Sento les vostres veus de joc a la placeta. No sóc orb, però em resteu invisibles. Veniu: amb tres rodes i un cordill li he farcit les entranyes i aquesta nit batrà les ales. Joan, Ernest! No voleu jugar més amb mi?

Ja el vespre es descompon en una escampadissa de fulls de paper de seda. Tot sol aniria a provar el mecanisme enginyós; però aquell capatàs m'ha dit que no em mogués d'aquí, i que aguantés hores i hores aquesta llarga barra de ferro, l'ombra de la qual, en projectar-se damunt la mar, s'hi insinua amb irregulars corbes obscenes.

It is I who carry, higher than everyone else, the huge aluminum bird we place atop the quarry fountain on moonlit nights. Pere! Lluís! Where are you? I hear your voices at play in the square. I am not blind, but you remain invisible. Come on out: I have stuffed the bird's guts with three wheels and a piece of string, and tonight he will beat his wings. Joan! Ernest! Don't you want to play with me anymore?

Already the evening decomposes into a scattering of sheets of tissue paper. I would go try the ingenious mechanism on my own. But that foreman told me I shouldn't budge from here, and for hours on end I had to hold this long iron bar. Its shadow, cast over the sea, insinuates irregular, obscene curves.

És inútil que, de cara a la natura com m'aconsellen els llibres, cerqui l'arbre on adés inscriví el teu nom o els pins que havien ombrejat els nostres jocs adolescents. Si estenc en creu els braços, topo amb els murs d'un túnel sense fi; si els alço enlaire, me'ls empresona una espessa cortina d'ales. Només quan en la meva desesperança cloc els ulls, la natura em somriu: prats, rierols, pollancres, fontanes i ocells viuen de llur vida encesa i es rendeixen a l'encís de les teves danses. Occiria el monstre que m'ullprengué, si les meves mans no fossin el record vague de dues fulles mortes, si el meu cos no fos una fràgil figuració vegetal.

In vain do I search, confronting nature as books advise me, for the tree where I inscribed your name not long ago or the pines that shaded our adolescent games. If I extend my arms to form a cross, I collide with the walls of an endless tunnel; if I raise them high in the air, a dense curtain of wings imprisons them. Only when I close my eyes, in my despair, does nature smile at me: meadows, streams, poplars, springs, and birds subsist on their glowing lives and surrender to the charm of your dances. I would slay the monster that captivated me, if my hands were not the vague memory of two dead leaves, if my body were not a fragile vegetal image.

Vindré més tard demà

—Vindré més tard demà. Em fa por de trobar ta mare, com cada vespre, a cada portal del teu carrer, amb una disfressa diversa: ahir, asseguda a l'entrada de la carnisseria, tota de negre, en passar jo, alçà els braços enlaire per dibuixar amb llur ombra, damunt l'ala vermella de la porta, no sé quin ocell malèfic; dues portes més amunt, a l'escaleta del veterinari, em mostrava impúdicament el si rugós, m'amenaçava amb lúbric esguard i, en veure'm fugir, se'm presentà, en tombant la cantonada, vestida de gran senyora, per provocar la meva sorpresa, dues cases més amunt, en un llindar equívoc, on darrere un taulell improvisat oferia, a poc preu, carotes i caretes diabòliques. A les trenta-tres entrades que precedeixen la de casa teva, ta mare, en fer-se fosc, se'm presenta amb un vestit divers i un maquillatge esporuguidor. Vindré més tard, vindré molt més tard. Passada mitjanit, ta mare, amb les altres dones del veïnat, miola per les teulades per desvetllar l'eco esgarrifós que agonitza al fons de les xemeneies. Tu i jo aleshores, darrere el mur de desferres rovellades que jauen darrere l'hort, contemplarem, callats, com s'amaga la lluna darrera la negra muntanya inaccessible que tanca la vila. Més alta que l'Himalaia, ningú no n'ha explorat encara l'altre vessant. Tot just el disc pàl·lid morirà en el nostre horitzó per a renéixer a l'altra vall, escoltarem el xoc de les llances amb què milers de guerrers saluden l'alba nocturna.

I'll Come Later Tomorrow

—I'll come later tomorrow. Every evening is just the same: I'm frightened to find your mother in a different disguise at each door in your street. Yesterday, as I passed by, she was sitting at the entrance of the butcher's, all in black, her arms raised in the air, their shadow sketching some malign bird I couldn't recognize across the red wing of the door. Two doors down, at the veterinarian's stoop, she was shamelessly baring her wrinkled breast, threatening me with a lewd glance, then, seeing me bolt, she appeared as I turned the corner, dressed like a grand senyora to shock me, then, two houses farther down, she turned up in a blind doorway, where behind an improvised counter she was offering diabolical masks and vizards at a cheap price. As night falls, your mother appears wearing a different dress, frighteningly made-up, at each of the thirty-three doorways preceding the door to your house. I'll come later, much later. After midnight, your mother, along with the other neighborhood women, miaows from the roofs to awake a bloodcurdling echo that wails in the depths of the chimneys. At that point, behind the wall of rusty debris lying behind the garden, you and I shall silently contemplate how the moon hides behind the inaccessible black mountain that seals off the town. Taller than the Himalayas, and no one has yet explored the other slope. The pale disk will die on our horizon only to be reborn in the next valley, when we shall listen to the clashing lances of a thousand warriors saluting the nocturnal dawn.

On aniré tot sol

Vaig aconseguir que em deixessin ésser pintor de parets. Dret, dalt un tauló sostingut per dues escales, pinto rètols a totes les cases: COTILLAIRE, COTI-LLAIRE, COTILLAIRE, COTILLAIRE. L'olor del vernís m'embriaga tant, que, a mig matí, deixo la feina i, presa d'una folla joia, corro carrer amunt i carrer avall, i crido *oia! oia!* Però el flequer que m'havia contractat ahir, em perseguí llanterna en mà fins a la placeta i m'obligà a acabar la T del rètol de casa seva. Era fosc, fosquíssim. Sense moure'm de dalt de la bastida em vaig posar a tocar valsos sentimentals amb un violí. Les acàcies havien plegat ja les branques damunt les soques i la pica de la font, somorta, engolia pètals marcits d'estel. Del fons misteriós del garatge de l'amo sortí, empesa per tot d'infants, i de la grandària d'una roda de carro, la lluna. Els ocells, a milers, brollaren del fons de les xemeneies i li volien buidar els ulls.

(*Jo també hi vull ésser! Jo també hi vull ésser!*, hauria cridat de dalt estant si els llavis m'haguessin obeït.) D'un bot salto a terra, m'entrebanco i caic. Els infants m'insultaven i em llançaven, furiosos, grosses boles de neu. (*Jo també hi vull ésser! Jo també hi vull ésser!*, hauria cridat si la veu no se m'ofegués sempre, Déu meu, sempre.) Quan els vaig voler atènyer, havien desaparegut darrere els velluts blau de nit amb què els veïns del meu poble amaguen els cancells de llurs cases.

Sola, immensurable, la lluna havia estat abandonada al mig de la plaça i projectava, en con, la seva ombra damunt una llarga planxa d'alumini. M'hi vaig voler acostar per empènyer-la, però un fred intensíssim em glaçava les mans. De les canaleres dels teulats saltaven, monòtons, rajolins d'oli. Al fons del carrer més baix una mà fosforescent es movia en pèndol.

(On aniré tot sol!: reprendria la tonada dels meus valsos, si m'hagués restat cap corda al violí; trucaria al Ton del bar . . . Però só geperut i, de dia, la gent del carrer riu quan passo i diu que só boig. Demà de matí em

Where I Shall Go All Alone

I was granted permission to be a wall painter. Standing atop a plank supported by two ladders, I paint signs on all the houses: CORSETIER, CORSETIER, CORSETIER, CORSETIER. The smell of varnish makes me so drunk that by midmorning I leave work, and, seized with mad joy, I dash up one street and down another, shouting *Oy! Oy!* But the baker who hired me yesterday followed me as far as the square, holding a lantern, obliging me to finish the T in the sign on his house. It was dark, pitch dark. Without moving from the scaffold, I began to play sentimental waltzes on a violin. The acacias had already folded their branches over their trunks, and the basin of the muted fountain was swallowing shriveled star-shaped petals. The moon, about the magnitude of a cartwheel, appeared from the mysterious depths of the boss's garage, pushed by a throng of children. Birds by the thousands burst from deep in the chimneys, wanting to empty his eyes.

(*I too want to be here! Me too!* I would have shouted from above if my lips had obeyed me.) With a vault I jump to the ground, stumble, and fall. The children were insulting me and furiously hurling huge snowballs. (*I too want to be here! Me too!* I would have shouted if my voice didn't choke every time I tried, my God, every time.) When I wanted to reach them, they would vanish behind the night-blue velvet that the villagers use to hide the vestibules of their houses.

Solitary, immeasurable, the moon had been abandoned in the midst of the square, and it cast its cone-like shadow over a broad sheet of aluminum. I wanted to draw near in order to push it, but a most intense cold froze my hands. From the rain gutter drops of oil leapt monotonously. At the end of the farthest street a phosphorescent hand moved like a pendulum.

(Where I shall go all alone! I would resume the air of my waltzes, if I had any strings left on my violin. I would ring Ton from the bar. . . . But

95

venjaré . . . Amb un carbó que tinc dibuixaré una ratlla a la paret de totes les cases, començant per la barraca dels burots i acabant per la rectoria. A la torre del portal nou de la carretera pintaré un rètol que dirà COTILLAIRE i, tot posant-me el barret ben de cantó i amb un pot de vernís a cada mà, m'amagaré darrere l'atzavarar de cal Canet per a escoltar al fons de mi mateix les cançons que em sangloten a la gorja i que moren a flor de boca.)

I am hunchbacked, and during the day everybody laughs when I pass by, and they say I am mad. Tomorrow morning I shall take my revenge. . . . With some coal in my possession, I shall draw a line on the wall of every building, starting with the municipal offices and ending with the rectory. On the tower of the new gate in the road I shall paint a sign that says CORSETIER. While wearing a hat cocked just right and holding a pot of paint in each hand, I shall hide behind the row of agaves at Can Canet, listening deep down inside myself to the songs that sob in my throat and die on my lips.)

Omitted Texts

J. V. Foix's first two book-length publications, *Gertrudis* (1927) and *KRTU* (1932), were miscellaneous collections that contained prose poems and narratives, a sonnet, verbal portraits of contemporary painters, an essay that addressed his motives for writing, even a letter that took issue with how a "friend and colleague" had responded to his work. From these diverse texts he selected a relatively small group of prose poems to form the section of "primers fragments" ("early fragments") in his 1981 edition of the *Diari 1918* (*Daybook 1918*). The texts that he omitted are presented here in English translations.

Gertrudis

I abandoned my horse. He lowered his eyelids in the most beautiful way, transforming the sun into an ornament on his forehead. I was mindful that he might carry me off into the night—a singular lantern which had guided me faithfully to Gertrudis's garden.

Seated on a bench numbered in red to accord with the red number on my ticket, my beloved hummed my name to the charming cadence of a popular foxtrot. The languor of a desire that had yet to be tested by the first kiss tempted me to open my arms and embrace her body—plainly mad. The mistletoe offered by a clear ray of moonlight stayed my hands in their eagerness to touch, and I needed to slip on some rubber gloves to immerse myself fully and reach her coveted gaze. This effort, preempting the joy from the kiss, proved to be enervating, stopping me from resuming the dialogue that a maid's groan had interrupted the previous night. She was emptying the footwarmer where I had gotten into the habit of resting my feet to keep alive the embers that failed me in the most intense heat.

In my amorous weakness I saw only Gertrudis's hair, and in clumsy words I praised the perfection of her braid. The powerful scent of the acacia narcotized us to the point of fainting. Successfully exerting my will, however, I gathered the scent in its entirety and enclosed it in a box fastened with a ring of authentic dragonite. I suddenly felt revived through a daring escape. With my right arm I encircled Gertrudis's sublime body, and with my bold gaze I sought in hers an eternal pledge.

The sky descended to blanket us, and the neighboring mountains, enlarged by the darkness which increased their bulk, created a fine enclosure by limiting the horizon in such guise that my lament resounded as in a cavern, and the firmament exhaled as if the universe had been reduced to our pleasurable retreat.

Gertrudis, careless of my affection, unfastened the stars one by one and with the thrill of infinity rinsed them in a silvery green marsh. She was handing them to the toads which, once acknowledged, initiated an odious clamor that I hastened to harmonize through a system of pedals furnished by my provident beloved.

With the ceiling clean of stars, I once more attempted a true possession of Gertrudis when an instinctive jolt led me to apply the telephone receiver to my ear to listen to a nightingale's graceful song. My face mellowed as the freshness of a cloister of nuns was transmitted over the line with voluptuous longing.

The moon, inflated to bursting, hung over us in heavy menace, and its extreme brightness softened the bench of our disport until it turned elastic. We were obliged to take refuge in a neoclassical temple and seek the help of my horse-lantern to escape, freeing ourselves from that mollifying cheat.

Somnambulant by inheritance, the horse appeared with his eyelids closed and plunged into the darkness. I spurred him with the point of a stylus, oiling his harness and moistening his eyes with the stimulating black bitumen that trickled from a mound. Heartened, we rode with Gertrudis and skirted an abyss when an exhalation from a bramble patch, rendering me ductile for a third time, decanted my brain so that I might reach the unattainable benefice. Cured of chronic amnesia, I remembered that Gertrudis, whose virtues I had found synonymous with the rhetorical trilemma, had been seduced by a black man at the stairs of the market in Sarrià. I myself had witnessed it while clutching a golden basket for the stranger. It was brimming with the scarlet stridency of crayfish.

This memory awakened an ancient jealousy in me. I brusquely took hold of Gertrudis, and I realized, emphatically, that she was nothing but a handful of perfumed rags: I threw her over a precipice. Dislocated by terror, I heard a dying person's lamentation expressed as the last spasm of a damaged gramophone disk.

After freeing the horse from my servitude, I walked aimlessly, astonished by the awareness that I felt no remorse. I was placid, verging on the serenity I needed to search for a carriage to return home.

Upon turning a corner in an unknown village, morning surprised me with the joyful opening of blinds. A line of district officials opened the dew taps, and soon a downpour caused me to fret about an almost immaterial yearning. Faced with this disquieting spectacle, I felt volatilized. The streets were sliding beneath my feet, and God exulted—when I saw a woman hanging Gertrudis's two braids beneath a balcony as if advertising a common transaction.

Melancholy denied me until I rediscovered the cretin I had been just now! Crumpled, frayed, I took recourse to the supreme electuary: purifying myself by sucking up the smoke from nearby chimneys. Thus I was disfigured in a peculiar way: my body had become an infant's, but my head retained its flighty twenty years. A mental agility situated me at the demise of human passions while a corporal agility allowed me to surrender myself to the greatest pleasure: shrinking from the pace of pedestrians but seeking refuge beneath the crust of great cities to grasp the melody that their robust steps intone as an offering to my meagerness.

Christmas Story

Why was that absurd bloom of poppies at the height of the walls, beyond reach? Every passage was closed, and I would have had to replace the switchman to be able to speak to him. But where was the railroad? Where were the trains? At the house on top of the hill they were holding a ball that evening because it was Sunday. The balcony of the Carlist center was filled with men wearing three-cornered hats, and the rector had a broad purple flag hung from the bell tower. The first star was wavering among the stage sets, and we had emptied all the wine into the road. But you should not fear any reprimand: I had become so emaciated and was clothed in such rags that not even you would have recognized me. I had thrust the dagger, of course, into the gate at the back of the garden. Dance! Dance! If your mother had given me the key to the attic, I would have roared with laughter at you and the president of the Society. There I keep the coat of mail, helmet, shield, and lance, and on the walls are drawn thousands of virgin continents and countless unexplored seas.

The ball must have ended early. At the top of the hill only the century-old rubble of a castle could be seen, and on the deserted horizon the man with the saxophone had just passed by, quickly, hurling his deep sounds, moving me, and making me vacillate between the two wooden crossbeams I was straddling, feeling like some cinema hero. At that point, I ran into my neighborhood night watchman who was sporting a splendid uniform as if he were working the most important festival, although with the huge keys, lantern, and lance he carried every night. He told me he would accompany me because the road was long and easily lost. I heard the noise of voices and hearty laughter, which I believed came from revelers who were heading home, but it was in fact caused by hundreds of night watchmen, decked in festival garb like the one from my neighborhood and laden as well with their nocturnal gear. The hilltop was crowned not by any ruined castle, which I had imagined to be the site of the ballroom where my darling spent her evenings, but rather by a gloomy barracks for carabiniers. The watchmen all looked and carried themselves in ways that made them identical to my companion, and they left the fragrant trail of a chromium lithograph.

Where could you have gone to spend the evening, Gertrudis?

We embarked on the road together, almost trotting. The moon favored the asphalt, abandoning the thousands of veils with which she vainly covers her nakedness. At a turn in the road, amidst the anticipation of the hundreds of colleagues who followed us with a great din of keys, lances, and hobnailed boots, my guide asked me: "Will you lodge tonight in Molins de Rei, sir?"

When I heard myself addressed with such respect, I trembled with weakness. Just the day before, after crossing the Diagonal, a man had tapped me on the back to say: "Listen, lad."

I felt very small before that man who addressed me respectfully, and I felt cold, very cold. The watchman promptly covered me—what a surprise!—with a heavy multicolored cloak I had given to Gertrudis as a gift. When I turned round to learn why our followers were bellowing such lively comments, I confirmed that the rustling came from some pine trees we had left behind, and my companion and I walked through the solitude of an unknown mountain. Instinctively I seized the watchman's hand: he increasingly seemed, in my eyes, more of a man. The noise of some carefully moved branches led me to glimpse the waiter from the bar, who was stealthily crossing back and forth, laden with long slabs of ice.

The stars were higher than ever. Why did my sailor's cap say PELAYO? Why was I wearing the short pants I wore as a child? Why was I so cold, so lonely? I started to weep. To comfort me, the watchman, who was of gigantic proportions in my eyes, jiggled his keys, lifted and lowered the lantern with the tip of his lance, and tried hard to cast a gentle look at me. Powerless to vanquish my fit, he began to sing old Christmas folk songs in a falsetto while strangely stamping his feet to accompany the rhythm. Then I noticed that at the summit of the mountain we were ascending there stood a palace with illuminated windows and enclosed gardens surrounded by very tall eucalyptus trees. Hanging from the eucalyptus, in the manner of Christmas trees, were toys with complicated mechanisms and unfamiliar uses, alternating with the other toys of my dreams (cars, sailboats, airplanes, dolls with multiple moving parts, boxes of chocolates, and so forth), tied to the branches with Scotch bows like those encircling the braid in Gertrudis's hair when I first saw her in the convent school chapel. Eager to reach the summit, I held onto the watchman's legs and dragged myself through the rubble.

"This isn't an illuminated palace at all," exclaimed my guide. "Nor are there toys in the eucalyptus trees. They aren't even eucalyptus. These are the gardens of the Palazzo Giusti in Verona."

"No," I observed. "It's the Villa Giustiniani in Padua."

"No, not that, either," replied the watchman. "It's the Temple of Karnak, and we're in the heart of Egypt."

Mentally I struggled to spell out the names of exotic cities and regions—Safed, Baalbek—and instinctively I recited them in a loud voice with a pronounced singsong rhythm: "Saratov, Sarajevo, Sasebo, Bashkir, Kirkuk, Kuban, Bangkok, Kodok."

The watchman closed his eyes and said: "No, no. Nak, Nak, Nak . . . Nagpur, Nak, Nak . . . Nakhitxevan."

I followed him: "Pp. No, before: Dj, Dk . . ." I had lost the meaning of the vowels, however, and was ignorant of their value, even their spelling.

We had reached the summit. We found no remains, whether of a palace or of a castle. There was nothing but the rudimentary frame of a shepherd's hut with four scraps that served as a cover, flapping in the wind like the four black pennants of a corsair. Facing the sky, amazed, we observed purple and silver filaments circulating madly through interstellar space, describing arabesques similar to those drawn in my pocket atlas for maritime currents—midnight blue and agonizing pink. On the sly from my companion, seized by strange emotion, I stashed among four stones an oil cruet I was carrying for some unknown reason.

While exploring the valley from the western slope of the mountain, we discovered a surprising spectacle. Over a vast expanse of sand, apparently the bed of a huge river, enormous carousels dizzily raised and lowered their unique chariots. Thousands of booths covered the valley, offering the ingenuity of the most singular games and sports. Circulating among them were the grotesque figures of mythological beings still uncatalogued, which competed against an apotheosis of rockets and fireworks weaving the most beautiful tapestry imaginable before our astonished eyes. Sweet music, emitted from indefinable instruments, was climbing from the profoundest depths of the abyss, where a moment ago the waters must have spread the edge of a mantle to canopy the maddest of sirens.

The watchman created half of a coconut shell with his right hand and fitted me inside it to undertake the descent. That was not a slope on a mountainside, however, but a waterfall gushing over a precipice, where, entirely on my own, I tried to row while tilting back in a canoe. At the base of the valley there appeared not some celestial Montmartre but wings that spread over the lofty pools in the outermost coves. The cold had frozen the unsteady stars, which surrendered, abandoning themselves to the snowflakes on the unattainable peaks sketched by the clouds.

The man with the saxophone again passed by, quickly, disappearing down a path. In vain I sought a Gold Flake and a match; in vain I tiptoed to seem taller. If I had had some tools, I would have forced open the door because the chill night frightens me. But who pays attention to a child?

I stretched out my hands to the shadows, and I felt revived by the presence of the architect Josep Francesc Ràfols. Bent by the weight of a bulky Mexican basket hanging down his back, from where little winged heads emerged, Ràfols accompanied the architect Antoni Fisas, who had darkened his face with charcoal dust so that he would more closely resemble a mixed-breed chief of Tahiti. Farther behind followed the painter Joan Miró carrying a briefcase loaded with celestial planispheres where he projected new constellations and modified the monotonous layout of the existing ones. Behind them were still more of my acquaintances, including the poet Sebastià Sánchez-Juan who was using a funnel as a megaphone to declaim his most recent poems.

So that they might notice me, I passed nearby and muttered pedantic names—Brunelleschi, Bloy, Pirandello, even Pythagoras—or "we Catalans." They did not recognize me. I searched through my pocket and produced a headline, the length of a palm, from a crumpled issue of *La Publicitat*. Nor did they see me. Dejected, I took refuge behind a column of tires and chucked on the ground the few aniseed sweets left in a paper cone. The man with the saxophone passed by again, and I dragged myself behind him. Here the watchmen fall in line, and here goes my guide. Here goes the garage we sought. Everybody goes down on their knees, and I try to sing, uselessly. Hosanna! I pull a priest from my jacket and tell him: "Do you see how Saint Joseph buttons his sport coat at the waist and doesn't wear the belt of his pants so high? Do you see how the Mother of God sits at his right hand, and I do the right thing to fall asleep every evening on that side?"

He did not respond to me, either. The noise of wings muffled my weeping. I slipped through the legs of countless worshippers and found myself in a mysterious courtyard. Small, insignificant, I contracted inside a box filled with eggshells. The cold was extremely intense. I wrapped myself up, as best I could, in a piece of sackcloth. As my sight faded, I saw a row of stockings shrivel up, hanging on a cord between two inaccessible mountains. My ear was attentive to the rustle of silk dresses and crimson petticoats caused by the stars in their career.

Where did you spend that night, Gertrudis?

"Deserted paths, lifeless thoroughfares"

Solo e pensoso i piú deserti campi
                    —Petrarch, *Rime sparse* 35

Deserted paths, lifeless thoroughfares,
shadows without shade by coves and sands,
ashes heaped in the maddest of bends,
trophies of love by windows and doors.

In what direction, madness, do you lead
this body of mine that fears no gales
nor is amazed by changing locales
and the thousand ghosts in towns that died?

I don't know the border in the dark land
that adjusts the act and the diverse step
for whomever solitude is good to breathe.

Is there any barracks or prison so hardened
or any galley in the perilous depth
that more enslaves me or sets me more free?

KRTU

As when she had walked in processions as a child, she was wearing a pink taffeta dress scattered with stars cut from tinfoil, a blonde wig encircled with a crown of natural roses, white mules with the monograms of Jesus and Mary embroidered in gold thread, and two flimsy, yellowed wings.

She was waiting for me in the air shaft, as always, between the sink, brimming with red soapy foam, and a lovely landscape of smashed tin cans and black containers of indeterminate use.

"Why have you worn such a long dress?" I would have asked her if I could have regained the power of speech. "One can't see the litmus of your knees, and on the dance floor I won't be able to take pleasure in your legs.

"Why does such thick foam cover the water in the sink? The paper boats can't sail, and even if I make every effort to remove it with the clothes washing paddle, we won't be able to simulate a rough sea."

She took me by the hand and silently led me down a staircase of uneven steps. Two stacks of railroad ties formed a refreshing passageway that was illuminated intermittently by tiny, cobwebbed lightbulbs. How much I thanked her for showing me my cherished landscapes with such attentiveness! Tunnels half dug, walled coastlines, subterranean galleries with groves of gigantic hoes and picks, utility sheds where a thousand ropes hang uselessly. More than Alpine panoramas or Pyrenean peaks, more than the wide pit and the natural cavity or cave, I delight in the untidiness of so many useless tools where the seductive rust sparkles like providential dew beneath the purplish light that my companion arranges here.

"Why do men praise mountains, forests, rivers, and streams but disparage — hypocrites! — the labyrinths they create in their metallic projections?"

In full interior monologue I didn't realize that we had reached the exit of a tunnel leading to a vast esplanade, where some men dared to externalize their divine aversion to nature while mimicking its disordered spontaneity with tubular figurations of lead and clay. Others tirelessly strewed the ground with baskets of graceful utensils from hardware shops. Farthest away, four men disappeared on the horizon, each of them laden with a hefty letter of the alphabet. Read together, the different letters spelt a mysterious name: KURT, URKT, TRUK, UKRT, TURK, KRUT . . . It belonged to the main character in my dreams.

"We shall be late to the ball," I would have said at that point if my speech had answered to my thought.

My companion was no longer at my side. Locked up forever in the vehicle that drives the three-phase generator, dressed in a ball gown fashioned from multiple layers of sky-blue gauze, she was withdrawing. At the same time, she bid me adieu with the smile of a thousand white daisies without lamenting the misfortune that condemned her to a prison so gloomy.

I, drawing ever closer to the ground, was reduced to an oil-soaked rag. I applied a pair of electric welding pincers to a metal support and illuminated the desolate valley with ineffable celestial lights.

Notes on El Port de la Selva

1

I was found lying in the sand when all the bathers had already deserted the beach. Stuck to my nape and back were papers of every color with inscriptions from customs authorities as well as from grand hotels and exotic spas. They wanted to pull the papers off of me, but what came away were pieces of living flesh.

2

Those two stones at Port de Reig, standing upright, scarcely touching, do not represent any Romanesque Virgin, as I believed, nor are they a hideout for pirates, as you believed. The other night I saw them move and project long phosphorescent trails upon the sea. I drew near: they were the two bloody hands of a monster shipwrecked two thousand years ago. At midnight, the fingers possess the transparency of crystal and reflect life at the bottom of the seven seas.

3

They fish for horse's eyes at the Cova Colomera when the clock strikes midnight. Only at that precise instant can the eyes be opened as you open an oyster. Their pupils float over a liquor so burning that no human lips could ever have approached it. In their depths is reflected the starry sky. Never look straight into them, because you will be seized by sadness without end, and a passion for coves where you cannot berth will bind your life to the most mysterious of destinies.

4

A raven's wings! What are so many barrels of tar doing in this place? A wing detached from Night has spread millions of black feathers over the most deserted sands, where my feet muffle their cry. No, it is Maria-Dolors's hair.

5

Last night, at the Café de la Marina, the fishermen swore: on the path to Cap de Creus, every Sunday afternoon, two women wearing empire dresses and silver mules walk over the raging waves, their eyes closed, their arms extended toward the northeast. Today, which is Sunday, we went there in Eusebi's boat, oars beating. But on the subdued sea, at the place indicated for the apparition, a light shone so intensely that we too were forced to close our eyes and extend our arms toward the northeast. When we opened them, it was pitch dark. Our feet were a weave of scales, and above the deserted horizon rose a star of immense coral.

6

I read: "Fish are created in the image and likeness of God. The fish in paradise want birds. After falling into the black waters of the wells of hell, they are drowned without ever dying. The human face resembles fish. God is fish."

7

Stretched out on the endless beach, I saw how the raging waves hurled a body identical to mine, in a fossilized state. I sought, in vain, to stand up. Pseudomorphized, my body was a dense fabric of stony snails, antediluvian clams, delicious bleached miniatures of animals that have grown extinct.

In the depths of rare interstices, a transparent membrane revealed marvelous underwater landscapes where the signs of the zodiac were floating luminous. Through the dark passageway crossing the rock Teiera, which facing east encloses the horizon, an extraordinary procession of monsters advanced: octopuses with camel feet, giants with horse heads, Herculean hands supported by the thinnest ostrich legs, eyes with phosphorescent corneas between enormous scaly lashes. If only the sea, transformed into a single black wave, might cover the entire earth! But the sea, in its transition at dusk, is a vast slab of onyx, whereon stars reflect their flaming red arteries and trace mysterious, inaccessible deltas.

8

The stars in the black night coil their incandescent fibers on the horned heads of the numberless horses that thunder down the beach. A tropical current drives the mad herd to plunge into the sea. At this hour, the sea is a mobile desert of black sand, impossible to tackle, and the horses let their eyes fall upon it amidst the loudest neighing. Darkness submerges the earth, and humans hear the noisy clash of a thousand crystalline bodies.

Introductions

Salvador Dalí

Only a few days ago, at the corner of my house, a dextrous adolescent holding a briefcase packed with books quietly offered me beautiful first editions: herbaria with chromo-lithographed plates, prolegomena to biology, naturist formularies, even celestial charts and atlases of historical geography depicting the stages in the mysterious formation and disappearance of the Atlantic continent. He was also carrying reproductions of the most singular images gathered from the platforms of the subterranean avenues of predream. Prepared to refuse the offer, I was surprised by his sudden disappearance just when he handed me an invitation to the opening of the Dalí exhibition at the Galeries Dalmau. The invitation was accompanied by a blank catalogue.

On these winter days, from six to seven in the evening, witches spread their broad variegated kerchiefs through the city streets and the seigneurial porters' lodges, and before uninhibitedly dancing the farandola in suburban squares, they pass unnoticed among the pedestrians with the sober noise of chimes, deep breaths, and furtive kisses, scattering in their wake that aroma characteristic of baked apples. Last Friday at that hour, heading up Passeig de Gràcia to Dalmau's, I hadn't quite determined that the adolescent from the previous day bore a rare resemblance to the painter Dalí, who he indubitably was, although his necktie was camouflaged and his eyebrows were ingeniously lengthened.

As I sought to enter the Galeries, however, I was intimidated by the realization that the porter was also the porter of the Cercle Eqüestre. I turned away, discouraged, when before me stopped the schoolgirls' car, which disappears down Carrer de la Diputació every evening amid clouds of satin and incense, leaving a trail of luminous carmine. They got out of the car two at a time, carefully folded their large artificial wings, and tightly knotted the wide bands of their neckties over their lips. The smallest girl, bringing up the rear, was dropping camphor balls in order to locate the way back. They cautiously disappeared in the shadow of the entrance as if penetrating the depths of a virgin forest.

I then established that the porter of the Cercle Eqüestre had been replaced by a long-bearded gnome who was making kind gestures in my direction, so I followed him. We heard our footsteps down the long passageway as if they might get lost in the vast rooms of another floor. On both sides of the corridor, several huge glass cases, which had just now been lined with books and more books, displayed extremely rare models of dissected birds.

"And so, Senyor Dalmau, are you really renovating your Galeries?"

Upon entering the exhibition space, Dalí was stroking a multicolored bird perched on his left shoulder.

"Superrealism?"

"No, no."

"Cubism?"

"Not that, either. It is painting, if you please, painting."

He showed me the windows of the marvelous palace he had constructed at Dalmau's. I had the distinct awareness of being present at the precise moment that a painter is born. The vivisection lecture hall showed vast physiological landscapes stripped of flesh: beautiful bloody groves shaded brief pools where fish struggle from dawn till dusk to rid themselves of their shadows. Deep in the pupils of the painter, of the harlequin, and of the mannequin were black stars falling in a silver sky. I was thinking of staying there forever when the hour struck seven and the famous ghosts issued from the depths of every canvas.

It is a beautiful spectacle: subtle, they cover you with their veils and infect you with their immateriality. If many Barcelonans were to know of it, the spectacle of the ghosts that fill Dalmau's rooms every dusk would be a unique opportunity for them.

As I quit the Galeries, the Passeig de Gràcia—deserted, treeless, without lights—was an immense avenue lined with hundreds of Shell gas stations, their luminous façades reflected sweetly on the asphalt. A will superior to mine made sure that, instead of following my route home down Carrer de Provença, I would take refuge at the service station on Carrer d'Aragó.

Joan Miró

I was surprised that, in mid-April of 1928, the exit to the tunnel at the Sant Gervasi train station was obstructed by the presence of a group of women dressed in green with hats and shoes of the same color in the style of the 1890s. I was also surprised that each of them ostensibly displayed a lithograph while contemplating it with indecipherable gestures. It showed a life-size reproduction of *La Gioconda*. ("*Mona Lisa! Mona Lisa!*" a railroad inspector bellowed at me. "No, *La Gioconda!*" I responded desperately. "*La Gioconda!*" We were on the point of coming to blows.)

That inspector seemed quite brawny. He wore an immense moustache which exactly reproduced typographic "moustaches." (I recognize you: in 1918 I saw you painted on the walls of the Galeries Dalmau, Carrer de la Portaferrissa. Then Joaquim Folguera assured me that you were the husband of a woman who always dressed in green. You're an imposter! You're nothing but the husband of every one of these ladies—who already number thirty, thirty-eight, forty-nine, ninety-seven, one hundred—and you've grown a moustache like Joan Miró's. You are neither an inspector nor Miró. But, my God, what if you were the painter Miró, husband to every one of these ladies? Miró, however, shaved off his moustache a while ago. If you weren't wearing these whiskers, I would say you are Miró. You are wearing neither an 1898 moustache nor a 1928 moustache; you are not clean shaven, inspector; you are not the husband of every one of these ladies. You are Miró, it is certain, Joan Miró, the painter Joan Miró. How goes it, Miró? How are you—forgive me—and each of your wives? Why have you let so many whiskers grow every which way on your face? Are you trying to multiply yourself as husband to each of your wives?)

The train, two carriages bound for Sarrià, finally passed through the tunnel. I continued my dialogue alone when I noticed that Miró was sitting at my side, sleeping as if for an eternity. As I attempted to wake him, his head mysteriously disappeared through the window in the shape of a phosphorescent egg. From the decapitated trunk issued a flight of birds in a column, and into my lap fell an enormous, gelatinous hand, as if a medium had materialized M. A. Cassanyes's hand.

When I believed I had reached the temporary station at La Ronda, I witnessed thousands of phosphorescent eggs ascending and descending along the shore of an unknown sea, floating restlessly through the atmosphere. I was on the verge of crushing several between my hands, giving birth to the beautiful unpublished worlds they carry in embryo, but my arms were the fallen branches of a dead trunk projecting over the landscape a strangled shadow.

Artur Carbonell

I found him in the middle of ornery March on the same beach, Sant Sebastià. He was dressed like an angel in a tunic of white silk, excessively long, decorated with irreproducible gold filigree. He covered his head with a luxuriant red wig fastened snugly by a diadem of daisies, and he wore his lips painted with the same magnificent sky blue secreted from his eyes. A solitary angel on a deserted morning, close to the sea, inevitably exalted my imagination. The banner with the effigy of Sant Bartomeu—which I spend the entire day walking from the town hall to the parish church—I left leaning uselessly against a wall, I readjusted the cincture of my surplice, and I approached the unfamiliar child. Never before that moment had I addressed anyone by suddenly using that sweet schoolyard language game: "Ou'reyay Arturway Arbonellcay, aren'tway ouyay?" He drew both wings into his breast and with a low reverence responded: "Esyay, Iway amway!" We shook hands and, at the distant shore, sifted sand through the entwined fingers of our two hands. I asked him: "What're you going to do when you grow up?" His entire response was to inflate his cheeks as much as he could. Then he asked me: "What about you?" Ashamed of my thirty barren years, I unbuttoned my cassock to show him my Adam's apple, quietly, with my finger, as it rose and dipped dizzily. We never said another word. Occasionally I give him the fourteenth line of a sonnet to read. His entire commentary is to inflate his cheeks. Then on canvas he draws and paints a breast for me (belonging to Matilde, Enriqueta, Josefina). My entire response is to point to my prominent larynx. Only when, occasionally, we run into one another in Sitges, I walking the banner of Sant Bartomeu and he dressed as an angel, gathering sea scallops and snails, can we repeat our names with amicable delight: "Arbonellcay!" I begin. And he responds: "Oixfay." Then once again we entwine the fingers of our two left hands and sift sand.

Applications

How absurd: they told me that I had to address you, that at the precise hour when sun, sea, and flesh weave dense arborescences and our ghosts wander through this miraculous forest, I must deliver a soliloquy without mentioning that I alone face a few dozen mummies who suffer the tragic condemnation of resisting the worm for eternity. You are not, by any means, unknown to me: I have seen you in funeral processions at the entrance to the parish church or inside your rheumatic chambers, stretched out on mysteriously covered sofas. I can, however, imitate your countenance, if need be, and my skin, taut as yours, enfolds me in a propitious mask, enabling me to behave with the imbecility of someone who speaks so that a look-alike might listen to him. That is the height of absurdity. Everything I shall try to communicate to you, uselessly, is made intelligible to our joyful shades by a flash in the eyes radiating through clouds, guiding us through the forest that our fleshly figurations have deserted. My pedantry will therefore be humble enough to recite only the texts of others. In the zigzag of white spaces introduced between one paragraph and the next, between one author and the next—Oh, my fellow mummies!—perhaps you will find the many indentations that reveal the route taken by my Philips radio.

1

An oversized roller unwinds, before my eyes, thousands and thousands of meters of black gauze. That portrait hanging on the wall: I shall never be able to set it straight again. Is it Blake? Lenin? My father at thirty-five?

2

Through a dense forest of deflated tires I managed to touch his shoulder. His eyes are glass, and his beard is curled like the beard on the *gegant* at Poldo's place in Solsona.

3

A sofa on a riverbank is a marvel. A man, bent beneath the weight of a huge R, advances slowly, sets down the initial on the sofa, which totters and falls into the river. But the river is glass, and it is broken into an uneven crack that runs from one bank to the other. If I lay down to feel its thickness with my hand, it would draw blood. A voice shakes the poplars to their roots, as if they were stage props, and it intones with immense clarity, *Marta!* Simultaneously I repeat the name. (Was mine the only voice to have shouted it?) That R had to be an M; it *is* an M. No, it is an R. If only the man who brought it would return! But he does not dare turn up because he is in shirtsleeves and the curtain is raised.

4

If the Ford weren't such a wreck, we'd take it for a spin and try it out. It has no wheels! All the same, Ernest Maragall hangs a ceramic angel on the radiator, its outstretched arms holding a scroll that reads, GLORIA IN EXCELSIS DEO. It isn't really a Ford; it's a Mathis, the 717171. If it manages to start, we'll go and pick up Feliça (?), Maria Pepa, and Niup (?). There's a ball at the Atheneum in Sant Gervasi. But we're completely naked, and Maragall, shaking my head as if he wanted to strangle me, keeps on saying: I've never worn a suit jacket! I've never worn a suit jacket!

5

—It certainly isn't a horse. In the vines, you say? But the sea is so hairy that the neighing moon can only be heard, at midnight, below the tunnels of the Garraf.

6

The Man-Who-Sells-Coconut has put on a false moustache so big that it made me weep with fear. He seized my hand and had me enter at the back of the stable where the black horses sleep. So that I would hush up, he showed me, through a cobwebbed chink, the vague landscape where a thousand silver rivers die in the sea, and he filled my hands with olives.

Letter to a Friend and Colleague

Distinguished friend and colleague:

I must resolve an ambiguity: your reading of my prose, which you compare to "a row of inspected gloves spread out in a dry cleaner's loft," has engendered a doubt in you. Like so many other, less beloved readers, you suspect that my literary production is an inept maneuver to dissimulate, beneath a shower of shavings, my shamefully unburied body. But I, who am so indifferent to the opinions of others, shall be frank with you, the most subtle of my friends and colleagues.

No, the place where the old blind servant sojourns is not behind the pine forest. In the chamber next to my bedroom, she makes her daily appearance, bandaged from head to foot like a mummy, arms stretched forward, hands open.

The corridor walls are marble, certainly, and the voice that shouts my name is louder every evening. But if I thrust my head out of the window, nobody, from the deepest cellars, responds to my desperate signals. And when the black column of birds advances from the west, making the shadow of night so frightful, earth and sky metamorphose into morbid velvet where my voice is muffled and my cries founder.

I predict, however, that an immense clarity will force so many presumptuous shadows into a disorderly withdrawal. Meanwhile do not fear for me. On the far, deserted avenue that I glimpse from here, a solitary barrel projects its divine shadow on the asphalt. And if I shake, I am immersed voluptuously in a thousand drops of tar, which remind me that the fluff of my body has still not been definitively plucked off.

Essays

Between 1917 and 1936 J. V. Foix distinguished himself as a prolific contributor to the Catalan press, both little magazines that proved ephemeral and daily newspapers with wide circulations. In hundreds of articles, he addressed a broad variety of topics that ranged from the most innovative trends in art, literature, and philosophy to far-reaching social and political developments. His focus fell on the present, yet he encompassed local, national, and international events. He gave special attention to the changing political situation in Catalonia from a nationalist perspective, and he occasionally commented on the cultural and social implications of his own writing. The essays presented here show him surveying the contemporary scene in which his first books appeared.

Avant-gardism

In the last issue we signaled avant-gardism as one of the factors that disrupt the stylistic elevation of our language. In the present article we shall try to clarify as far as possible what is offered to the avid reader under this term, along with the risk to our renascent literature that, in our view, may derive from excessively consulting authors who are adherents of avant-gardism.

Before anything else, we must make public a particular inclination of ours, a curious liking and—in certain cases—an ardent affection for the various conflicting manifestations of foreign avant-gardist tendencies. We have contributed a trivial collaboration, moreover, and we have even made a vehement apology among hesitant colleagues. Need we remark, then, that the same investigative spirit that led us to exotic vagabondage and extravagant expression in the red expansion of our infancy leads us today to make a number of retrograde considerations? Need we simultaneously exonerate ourselves and repeat that in both cases love of truth and of Catalonia has been the main engine of our divergent actions?

Not long ago, Carles Soldevila, who has a fine reputation as well as a fine spirit among contemporary youth, indicated that Catalonia's actuality as a nation could be demonstrated by means of a Futurist approach. We may lose interest in whether Catalonia was once a distinct nation and rather demand its right to construct itself as such with time. Have you considered the vast horizon that this concept of nationality extends before our eyes? Does not your soul burn, do you not feel renewed as if your life were transmuted, as if some new blood were flowing in your veins, as if your muscles were newly articulated?

Like a virgin inclined to marry, a nation under construction figures the world before it as a fairy meadow where Madness and Immortality sojourn and comfort untiringly. It exalts the youthful imagination, tempts all our activities, feeds our lyricism with intensity—imagining a new homeland, only just born, drives our creative gesture, possessing every vital attribute. In the face of this homeland, who will stand in opposition? In the bosom of this homeland, what injustice will be permitted? Consider: two, three, four million men—in the present instance, Catalans—proclaim in one unanimous chorus of wills their desire to constitute themselves as a nation. They do not want to know a thing about their past: what is history to them? Nor do they want to know anything about the regimes to which—until this moment—they have been subjected: free from atavisms, born, so to speak, with their homeland, they mutually agree to consider themselves equal before the sacred idol and to form a dense army facing the future. In a moment of divine intoxication, they even abolish every hierarchy and accept as their initial constitution the extreme statutes of the most advanced social and aesthetic theories in vogue throughout the world. They have built a perfect nation: the red flag and the flag of the Homeland are, in the end, the same thing. On the way to the future, the advance of Catalonia will possess an irresistible beauty. The example and name of our Homeland will become immortal in the face of the decrepit world and decaying empires.

Is not this the image that presents a Futurist conception of nationalism? And in art and literature, where lyric effusiveness will be absolute, is not this Futurist evocation also equivalent to the proclamations hurled at cosmopolitan interests by the new generations of vacillating tradition?

Situating ourselves before the current state of European literatures in their extreme expression, we affirm, in effect, a zeal, a will to renascence, a bold activity of exploration in the most conflicting directions: avant-gardists and classicists conduct foggy debates to bring about the renewal which has to lead them to an original rejuvenation. Both, however, in the clamor of proclamations, parties, tendencies, doctrines, and schools, reveal the truth to our eyes: their cause has passed; their situation is mortal. This yearning for renascence, this fever for research are symptoms of decrepitude.

Everyone must bear in mind that those who express themselves with the frankest clarity when they consider their fatal exhaustion are the lucid spirits of these decadent civilizations, these dying literatures. For them, the elapsed centuries of civilization have led to today's decline, and they affirm the existence of talent without genius, anarchy in ideas, and hopeless weariness. We are all acquainted with this sense of the situation in France. And what shall we say of Italy? Italian literature will perhaps never withstand the current crisis. Not long ago someone observed that this literature does not play any active or fertilizing role: it has transformed itself into a sad branch of French, English, and Russian literatures. French literature, however, provides only what translators consider exportable ("one passes from Rolland to Claudel, from Claudel to Apollinaire, from Apollinaire to Tzara . . ."), and Italian presses, just as happens in Madrid with Spanish presses, care to publish only the latest novelty of a literature tending toward ruin. We need not expect, therefore, any future for these literatures, and they can set no example for us, who claim to live in a veritable renascence.

Nonetheless, this common denominator in avant-gardists and classicists—zeal for renascence—is continually witnessed in the leading journals of these literatures. In both, the vision of a new classical age leads them quite often to use a common lexicon. And although in both a profound abyss separates the ethical from the aesthetic aim, the same result is still offered to our impartial intention: pastiche. In the former, a bloodless neoclassical pastiche; in the latter, a pastiche evocative of a future civilization that is nothing but the City of Memory, where the shades of vanished civilizations wander.

In a resurgent nation and literature like ours, understandably, the false renascence of dominant literatures might appear as a beautiful dawn, and the rash might try to imitate their extravagant manifestations. Every nationalism, on the other hand, contains a patriotic upstartism quite similar to the majority of avant-gardisms, which are characterized by their interest in drawing attention to themselves and in obtaining immediate glory. It is commonly said that a young people chooses philosophy that is basic and easy, and the truth is that several local manifestations of avant-gardism and pseudo-avant-gardism correspond to this observation.

Certain aspects of Italian Futurism, certain international manifestations of literary sub-Cubism are due precisely to a romantic explosion of upstartism. Let us focus on certain names printed exaggeratedly under the headlines of some publications. It might be said that the name has eaten the author and his work. The disproportionate exhibition of surnames leads one to suppose that the interpretation given to today's particular literary manifestations—as deriving from a fear of work—has guessed right. Such a publicist, who screams because he is incapable of syllabifying or who uses an acrostic or graphics because he is ignorant of written language, would see his ideal achieved if, over the darkness of the mansards in an urban square or competing with the stars one night, his name appeared inscribed in one of those electric advertisements of industrial propaganda. He would even like to see his measly poems scattered in a sudden blink across the darkness of the night sky. Moreover, some avant-gardists—although not all, naturally—have been observed to exalt ignorance, deny the value of work, express repugnance for effort, study, and, above all, useful learning, harmful only to the incapable. This fever to draw attention to themselves is, however, similar to that of the lower classes among the nouveaux riches, who are vulgar and uncouth. The outlandish, inferior jewel and excessive libertinage derive from a presumption equivalent to that of avant-gardist ballyhoo. In both we find the same level of ignorance, the same insolence.

It is curious to note that these whims of innovation, which in countries with an ancient national culture encounter reasonable resistance, are accepted straightaway in countries that lack a tradition or possess a false indigenous culture. And in these cases the spiritual deformation that the innovation implies in the collective generating it is evident along with every flaw. Should we land in Italy with dynamic, optimistic Futurism

132

(we would almost say national and militaristic), or in France with ecstatic, intellectualistic Cubism, or in Germany with pessimistic, defeatist Expressionism, we would find an explanation, a process, even a tragic movement of reaction against some dead thing that stifles every original expansion. But the nations that receive the alien creations later instead reveal a confusion of diverse tendencies and clumsy applications. Hence this profusion of variegated publications and this appearance of avant-gardist Esperantism, the manifestations of which reach us with such great frequency. The plastic Cubist and Futurist beautifully realized in particular circumstances in France and Italy, when displaced from their countries, are diverted to the opposite of their original direction. National avant-gardisms then become revolutionary, mystical, humanitarianistic, and even communist. In a good number of Swiss or similar publications, these extremes are accepted en bloc as if an ideological commonality existed among them.

It must be recognized that in Catalonia, where the spirit of construction is similar to the spirit of construction that drives the most serious Western avant-gardists, the effects produced by these fermentations have been slight. More precisely, a naïve joy, a patriotic idealism, an active commitment to contribute to the cultural reconstruction of the Homeland have given some superficial examples of avant-gardism to contemporary literature. The direct results are actually insignificant and inaudible. Yet not so the derivations that, lacking control and tending directly toward the mutilation of the language at the moment of its rehabilitation, could exert a dangerous influence.

It is said that in our time the worst of all enemies is ease. This enemy is acknowledged especially in countries with secular traditions and cultures. What will happen to Catalonia, where the secular is the interruption of tradition and culture? Let us bear in mind that this lack has led almost all of us to search for these elements of civilization in other countries, and that a number of our productions are equivalent to those of the adopted cultures, with the sole variant of being expressed in our language, victim of a foolishness that needs to be avoided.

Must we take our retreat so far as to deny ourselves every modern reading for the sake of our own health?

Some Considerations on Current Literature and Art

As time passes, the outcry of those who either demand sincerity from artists or deny it to them has become a vague, rippling murmur on which the subtlest canoes, powered by the most original oars and the boldest of rowers, float with benign indifference.

I have recently discussed the issue with my colleagues at *L'Amic de les Arts*—often and with insistence. We are definitely agreed that a distinction must be drawn between *sincerity* and *conviction* in art, following so many texts that have established the scope and difference of these terms, whether flexibly or with rigidity.

Still, this idea is nothing new: the unpublished flowerings of our spirit are no more than reproductions of those by which a centuries-old stem is eternally renewed in other, similar spirits. Hence we can clearly express our point of view as well as its *originality*. (I seem to have written this statement with a sinuous arabesque traced invisibly by the paragraphs of the ancient and modern authors we cite.)

The texts that refer to artistic sincerity and emotion are so numerous I feel it would be more economical to transcribe a discussion, however imperfect, which I conducted with several confrères along the Ronda de la Universitat.

* * *

In art and in literature—we said—a distinction between *sincerity* and *conviction* must be drawn. Hence the importance of giving emotional content to the word *sincere* and intellectual content to the word *convinced*. Normally, sincerity affects the sentiments: we are sincere when we state what we have experienced without dissimulation. Conviction pertains to the rational order: argumentation and proof, dialectic and logic. (Sincerity can affect ideas: on this point we agree. I can, for example, be sincere in stating my convictions.)

When I write my prose texts—most of which I am averse to accepting as Surrealist, since I attempt to fix images of a living reality—I behave sincerely toward myself and my reader. I am therefore sincere insofar as I communicate experienced situations without fraud. From a strictly literary point of view, furthermore, I would dare to affirm that I am true. Still, I am convinced, on the level of ideas, that this realism and this verism are not a universal reality. They are, in other words, neither the notion of Reality nor the notion of Truth.

We make all these considerations, again, from a strictly literary point of view. In the field of philosophy or, perhaps better, metaphysics, we would ultimately venture to pose them in other terms. If the notion of Reality involves that of Perfection, if, according to Spinoza, Reality = Perfection, if the reality that we attribute to a poem or a painting depends on its being more or less real within literary history, and if, as other philosophers prefer, Perfection is not humanly attainable, then the notion of Reality becomes for us a Superreality before which we find ourselves always in deficit.

No one can avoid the fact that I consider my prose texts to be realistic while demanding legitimacy for an appellative that has been appropriated by those who so delightfully cultivate infrarealism or the false copy of a reality, a human notion of reality, before which a great number stand with eyes closed and heart paralyzed.

In another vein, sincerity and conviction are simultaneously shared: the Catholic is sincere in his passions and in sin while being convinced of the irrefutable truths of the dogma which he professes, contrary to instinctual impulses.

* * *

I know that Salvador Dalí is sincere in his painting; I am unaware of whether he is convinced. Joan Miró, I know, is sincere and convinced. Exaltation in the former, bliss in the latter.

* * *

A common denominator can be signaled, perhaps, among so many motley groups, a single monochromatic flag above so many multicolored pennants: the struggle against what we called, generically, pastism. The most numerous armies have deserted this flag, which some still believe leads the battle. Pastism is not currently a fearful enemy, nor is it even the enemy. The dispersion or disbandment of the combatants has, however, brought some groups to dominance over others. Nowadays, for example, in France, an authentically advanced group remains as a result of all the commotion: the Surrealists, along with three or four independent writers who, every man for himself, have preserved their incontestable personality.

* * *

Although we deploy the term "avant-garde" and its derivatives to understand our situation, they strike me as a costly means to signify the post-symbolist movement. Especially given the erroneous use we have made of those words, as well as their truly indefinable meaning. As someone may have already remarked, the term "avant-garde" and its derivatives must be considered meaningless expressions in literature. If we actually want to consider this application, the existence of diverse literary avant-gardes must be admitted: Joan Maragall, for instance, was an avant-garde writer; however, the false avant-gardist Joan Salvat-Papasseit was not.

* * *

We whistle, despite ourselves, at Venus Anadyomene, rising from the sea, if she dares to appear naked in paintings; and we applaud, despite ourselves, the most deformed of her Ethiopian slaves.

* * *

French literary Cubism, in some of its aspects, is humanitarian, pacifist, internationalist. Italian literary Futurism has always been nationalist and fascist. We have frequently confused the two movements. Extreme French tendencies have been libertine from the beginning: when they fought for formal freedom (from free verse to the calligram), they frankly expressed their anarchic background, their fundamental lack of discipline. In those for whom avant-gardism was an intelligent game, an aesthetic pleasure, a manifestation of literary exuberance (Apollinaire), the derivations in the political and social order have been nil. Purely and exclusively literary, essentially mystifying, their juggling has been inoffensive and at times facetiously medieval. I believe that Apollinaire and his plagiarists have been the least avant-gardist of all their turbulent generation, however paradoxical that may seem. It was among the Dadaists that a true avant-garde emerged.

* * *

Naturally, for those who follow all the literary vicissitudes of recent generations, the accidents of a trajectory so crazy are important and often moving. They will be imperceptible, however, in future literary history. In short, it is a commonplace that only two or three names are retained from every school, reduced to a unity at the start of a century. Nowadays we distinguish the individuals within each group and the evolution of each individual in a particular period; we predict the immediate influence of a reading or of a spiritual trend on this individual. Later we will see only the tendency of the group, and, at the end of a literary epoch, a nebula that integrates a totality of tendencies will be visible. Nonetheless, in five hundred years or in a millennium, the most admired classic, the maestro, the immortal may be replaced by a facetious author of calligrams.

* * *

Hence the sensible critics, the dogmatic members of any academy who may wish to judge contemporary imaginative literature from their point of view and, if they are so condescending and liberal, who apply an arbitrary, extra-official dogma—they all run the risk of becoming laughingstocks. An adventurer of a new literature instinctively avoids all external critical control. In his asceticism, every human ambition is refused. Perhaps this is the extreme form of ambition. Perhaps it is the limit of an extreme pride. It is a fact, however, and it must be stated. Please apply an epithet to them: cynics. And you will still be confused, since using it in its current acceptation may enable its original meaning to be historically recovered.

* * *

In modern literary or pictorial explorations, we experience a very similar pleasure, certainly, with the speleologist Norbert Font i Sagué when along the shores of the Garraf he plumbs the depths of La Ferla sinkhole or discovers, in the Bruc sinkhole, a lake at the bottom of the last cave where no mariner has ever beaten his oars.

* * *

Romantics? Mystics? Both at the same time? Perhaps. Yet it is more justified to think that, without being one thing or the other, they relinquish themselves to a romantic or mystical experience, or alternatively both, with perfect lucidity. Their originality may be this: the great adventure of committing themselves to navigating, at full throttle or with propeller stalled, through the exceedingly vast firmament of the imagination, directionless, although with the prescience to end up unscathed.

✳ ✳ ✳

"If they could write a hundred Ronsardian verses, if they felt themselves capable of writing a Racinian act, if they authored a canto of the *Divine Comedy*, they would abandon their chimera," said a critic. No. If they were brought a masterwork of academicized literature they did not write in order to affix their signature to it, they would refuse, despite themselves. All past beauty is dead to their sensibility. They know that it was beautiful, that for a new generation it will be beautiful again, that it possesses an eternal value, that it is Beauty itself, Goodness itself, Truth itself. For them, however, it is a specter, and its memory or presence is annoying. This is Romanticism, quintessential but deliberate, aware, reasoned. For the formula Art for Art's Sake they substitute Adventure for Adventure's Sake or, if we accept the qualified notion of romantics that we apply to them, Romanticism for the Sake of Romanticism. The idealism that drives romantics, their humanitarianism, does not exist in modern imaginations. Before the great annoyance of existence, they surrender themselves to the most risky spiritual acrobatics.

✳ ✳ ✳

Art, like living beings (Lamarck), cannot avoid adapting itself to the conditions that are made for it. A so-called classic sculpture is, in the eyes of many, a ghost. The artist establishes an order in the period to which chance has assigned his life, and he does not dispose of more material than what he offers his epoch through diverse levels of spiritual and physical activity. He already does enough by building himself a cabin that is sufficiently ventilated to prevent him from dying of suffocation or spreading the plague with the putrefaction of his unburied body.

* * *

We shall advise them not to write. If their literature does not exercise the beneficial social function that has been assigned to it, if neither literature in its positive sense, nor art, has anything to do with that function, why so much wasted paper, so many useless books? Don't ask them. They will respond, if they appreciate you and wish to be polite, that they do it for sport. You will be dumbfounded. Who rows all alone on Sundays, out past the jetty, endlessly? Who runs enthusiastically, flying in vain over hundreds of kilometers without a fixed goal? Who wanders through space beating his wings, lacking an airport for landing? Or who submerges himself in the open sea for his own enjoyment? Does he surprise you?

* * *

No work is, in the final hour, useless. Less still boldness of spirit. Dadaism was an exercise in irresponsibility. Here you have the athletes who have most profited from it: the Surrealists. Leave them to their orgy: the neophyte's madness! Balance regained, they will discover a few images that are fresh and new, quite useful, and they will free the imagination from the dregs that infect it.

* * *

Psychoanalysts have been most interesting on this point: associations of images that appear to be highly absurd, disordered, and devoid of significance are revealed, through analysis, to be linked by a logic of the passions. With every precaution, after assuring himself of the integrity of the sense organs, Jaume Balmes said that the imagination is not limited to reproduction but rather forms ideal wholes to which reality does not correspond. Without this faculty, he said, mankind would not do anything new; it would be limited to copying the naturalness of a fixed and invariable manner. For Balmes, the fecundity of the imagination is at times independent of the will, demonstrating the existence of an order of faculties that are higher than the sense organs (*Metafísica-Estètica*, XV.122). Balmes also wrote that, when excited by sensory impressions, our spirit acquires the knowledge of incorporeal things (*Lògica*, I.I.12). Yet Balmes, with the play of calculated images, interprets idealism; Freud, with his images, interprets a certain reality; we, beyond what these others do, interpret Reality.

✻ ✻ ✻

The exciting problem is posed by our language and our literature. In a moment of reaction against my exacerbated sensibility, I proposed that we refrain from reading anything modern, suggesting it to myself. If the experiment were possible, we would need to prepare ourselves. All of us, however, would have to be prepared. It would be difficult for such a sensibility to avoid being refined by the most discriminating sensibilities of developed literatures while every other colleague continues writing in the manner of—precisely—the same modern and contemporary literatures. If our literature must still be a province with respect to other literatures, or the province of two or three particular literatures, it is useless to claim that we are influenced by a particular school or tendency while excluding the others. The immense sequestration must involve all or none. Our literary historians must signal the epoch in which our literature commanded its own original value. The data we have been given, perhaps imprecise, are hardly inspiring. I fear that "provincial" Catalan literature, now and in the near future, does not hold any immediate possibility of being liberated. In the background, clearly, there exists a political situation that carries in itself a possible solution. We share this point of view, especially those of us who believe that our radical originality will lie not in creating an autochthonous Art or Literature but in the realization of a Politics.

* * *

The manifestations—which are diverse and often opposed to the so-called avant-gardist group—have hardly ever been precisely nuanced in Catalonia. Futurism, Dynamism, Cubism, Dadaism, Surrealism, etc., are current expressions in our discussions. All the same, I have observed quite recently how difficult it is for anyone to distinguish them clearly. This difficulty of classification is a sign that we lack enough maturity to apply ourselves to contributing certain daring innovations. Just as a number of our purported poets are incapable of drafting a letter correctly, a number of avant-gardists find themselves in exactly the same predicament. When the person who constructs a sonnet does not know how to write a postcard, we can rest assured that the sonnet is even worse than four badly edited lines. Whoever writes verses without punctuation, or words in freedom, or enjoys composing a literary puzzle has to know how to write a sonnet correctly. The boldness, the innovations can be permitted only to exceptional temperaments. Several pastiches of avant-garde literature that have appeared in Catalan make us bow our heads in shame.

* * *

My prose texts or their equivalents possess an infrangible identical unity like that of the fourteen lines of a sonnet. The images they contain constitute a rhythm, and their consonance partakes of an academic rigor. No one can force me to suspect that the paintings of Dalí and Miró might lack that unity which absorbs or repels homogeneous or allogeneous elements with inflexible tyranny.

Some Reflections on One's Own Literature

When I published my first prose pieces in 1918, an illustrious critic for whom I feel deep affection asked me: "Why do you write *this*?" The question long decided the fate of various short texts—poems?—that I was writing in the form of a diary. Several appeared in *Trossos*, a magazine that disseminated avant-garde tendencies, founded by Josep Maria Junoy and edited by me for two numbers.

Why do you write *this*?—precisely. Not, Why do you write *in this manner*? Among my friends both questions have been raised, alternately. There were moments when I myself repeated them. Why write *this*? Why write *in this manner*?

The survey conducted by *Littérature* among young French writers in 1919–1920—"Why do you write?"—is sufficiently well known. Next to an imposing majority of pedantic responses, enough to discredit every literary work produced by their authors, a few, very few, were genuine. "Out of weakness," replied Paul Valéry. "Because . . . ," replied Blaise Cendrars. "To pass the time," replied Knut Hamsun. "That's what I ask myself," replied Jean Ajalbert. If a conclusion must be drawn from this survey, it is literary uselessness, equivalent to the uselessness of the artist. Alongside anti-painting, anti-literature. Weakness, indifference, misery, as opposed to their synonyms: scarcity, necessity.

Why do you write? Not the pedantic Why do you write *this* or *in this manner*? In rereading—what a heroic effort!—my first collection of prose (*Gertrudis*) and the poems that *L'Amic de les Arts* published uninterruptedly in every number over its three-year existence, I had to situate myself, with enormous difficulty, in moments of unusually frank optimism so as to hear once more the arguments that support my delusion about the legitimacy of printing my poetic periphrases (circumlocutions?)—even if in editions of one hundred copies. Although until now I have refused to deliver any of these fragile experiments to periodicals with a circulation higher than what is typical of sectarian publications, I doubt that I have imparted too much flexibility to my strictness. On the other hand, are we not always too *passive* before the uncontrollable voracity of people in an epoch that provokes our exhibition by every means?

If I confess my immoderation when faced with the thoughtful request of those who may be my best friends, it is because, in reflecting — also at their behest — on the origin of my spiritual position before the literary objectivation of my psychic states, of my indolence in avoiding that position, of my shamelessness in abandoning it in the middle of the street like an unserviceable shoe, a tin of tainted fish, or some discarded beans badly wrapped in newspaper, I must take as my point of departure the most intense moments of my adolescence, when I had promised myself that my hand would never sign my name, that I would be inexorable in realizing my personality, which I aspired to project, dematerialized, like a brief shadow that slipt over the sea, perceptible to the fish only for an instant, or over the calm autumn sky fleetingly glimpsed by a flock of birds.

In betraying this aspiration at a later age, in allowing that there might have been someone who wrote with conviction, in admitting my certainty that no one ever read my writing; in stabilizing the four consonants and two vowels of my false pseudonym; in stereotyping it correctly, I tempered my immodesty and consented to hurl myself into the abyss that my youthful ambition aspired to preserve in a silent flutter of wings.

For me, then, my literary production is a defeated protest, a phenomenon of spiritual dissociation similar to what men of science designate as the consequence of the death of an organism, with its bifurcation, total dispersion, even destruction. Total?

Gathering the three hundred prose poems I have written into three groups seems right to me. The first consists of those texts that best represent the *retreat (refoulement)* from that initial ambition: the vague, uncertain images, which play within a poem that is resolved in accordance with very strict norms, are a precise reflection of a violent propensity for all forms of moral and physical imperialism. In their realization, the classic phenomenon of intellectual liberation through the work of art is produced inversely: each new poem is a new element of intoxication which demands other poems with imperious exigency. It is a closed world whose irreal exoticism held me and whose prisoner I have long remained.

In the second group, I situate the poems and narrations that have permitted me an actual liberation in arranging arbitrarily those same images with the aim of disorienting their situation within the reality where they move or metamorphose. In intervening here, I had to avoid a double danger: that of entering unthinkingly into mysterious streets without end, where the weak get lost, and that of arriving at the discovery of the trick (which makes its possessors so famous) of producing serially and with *esprit*.

The third group represents a collection of *applications* composed in the light of day, with strong optimism and a love of risk which I like to regard as holding a strong sense of literary sportsmanship, uselessly generous if you like, insofar as I do not aspire to intervene into any competition and insofar as I refuse the championship. I consider some of these applications to possess an indisputable documentary value.

Of course, these groups do not contain frail and frivolous literary texts that remain—for example, "Pepa the Milkmaid" (see *Gertrudis*). I find it difficult to recognize them as my own.

I feel that lack of space does not permit me to situate in the social sphere the point of view I represent within Catalan literature. I take pleasure in saying, however, that I believe the position of some of our literature is loyal. This *retreat* from individual ambition is only the consequence of the retreat from a collective ambition. Within this vast lumber room, where many of us have to live, it is not strange that *disorder* might be, still, the only order possible.

Homeland

Every definition has served to justify the idea of a Homeland. Charles Maurras is right, from the central point of view of his ideology, when he elevates the Homeland to the category of absolute myth. Kliment Voroshilov is right when he declares, amid firing squads and exiles, that the Homeland must be served in the USSR. Romain Rolland is right when he shows that he is willing to die for a new Homeland. Maurras, however, defends the *nationalist* Homeland which, if we consider carefully, is precisely no other country but France. Voroshilov orders executions in defense of the *socialist* Homeland which, likewise considered carefully, turns out to be no other State but Russia. Rolland would die for a *universal* Homeland, in opposition to individual homelands, local or tribal.

This speculative play on the concept or notion of a homeland might be an unremarkable diversion if the participants who delight in it did not feel dissatisfied when they cannot proclaim their opponent's bloody annihilation. How easy it would be to ask the sufferer, the oppressed patriot or the starving wretch what "homeland" means to him! The sad fact is that the homeland of a Senegalese—who would admit it?—is France, the homeland of a Congolese is Belgium, and that of a Tagalog has been, indiscriminately, this or that great State in its imperial phase. Perhaps only people who suffer persecution for justice know how to define the idea of a homeland—if they could be honest.

In Italy, obviously, whoever attacks fascism opposes the homeland, in Russia whoever attacks Stalin, and in Germany whoever offends Hitler (even if the offense is just a look). A Croat, however, knows with certainty that he does not share the Serbian homeland, just as a man from the Empordà does not share the Andalusian or Irish homeland. Something must be at stake here. Yet so many distinctions, and with such subtleties, will draw out our commentary, and we will wind up forgetting that our task is to look past the spines of books.

In France, you can still avoid getting shot for swearing that not every Tom, Dick, and Jordi is the Homeland—a stroke of luck, if we give it any thought. Lately, however, some French are claiming that the idea of a Homeland is linked to the State, and this is everywhere. To be a patriot, according to them, you must be a nationalist and accept, as an article of faith, that the interest of the State, the reason of the State, and the truth of the State are above Freedom, Reason, and Truth, considered as universal categories.

Yet since in France, perhaps more than in other places, some idealistic writers do not believe in the existence of two kinds of justice, French and universal, or two kinds of truth, national and eternal, it is also the site where the cause of national egoism attracts the most savage supporters in persecuting anyone who defends the existence of universal values.

The group of editors and contributors at the journal *Esprit*, recently accused of joining the anti-France boosters, has collectively signed a manifesto, "Our Homeland," whose most emphatic paragraphs seem interesting to assemble. After attacking those who confuse politics with politicking, they say: "We know only one watchword: Truth, destroyed among adversaries, everywhere mixed with falsehood, from which we shall everywhere set it free. Never shall we be forced to think, write or work in accordance with the bloc that protects every idleness, every confusion, and every falsehood: right, left; Marxism, anti-Marxism; France, anti-France. We love our country. We love it in its merits and in its defects. We know that homelands possess the weakness of being incarnated, limited, partial in their gifts and in their affinities, and that even this weakness is a constitutive part of our affection for them. But we also know that your love for one being lasts long only if you love that being above yourself." To love the Homeland, France, does not mean to love it in its legal aspect but rather as an ideal. "In our view," they say, "Louis Malvy does not represent France, nor does Jean Chiappe, or the extortionate municipal council, or the conservative press, subventioned by the purveyors of war materials, or capitalism, concerning which a high, universal moral authority was able to write that your homeland is wherever your money is. This is anti-France. Right or left, we see it everywhere we see disorder. In opposing it, especially when it claims to exercise a monopoly on the homeland, we do not forget France: we work to recreate it anew."

The homeland, we have often written, is not the absolute. Nevertheless, the universal is given to mankind through particular figurations. The signers of the manifesto in *Esprit* swear that the more human and universal, the more diverse will be the revolution they are mounting. Only materialism, whether communist or nationalist, disfigures a country and individuals. If any leveling passion threatens us all at this moment, it is the new internationalism of totalitarian States closed on race, instinct, or vindications, an internationalism that, in destroying the meaning of individuality, disrupts physical unities.

They do not deny the Homeland, then. But the Homeland is not divine or sacred. It is positively not entitled to the exclusive cult, exaggerated devotion, martyrs, and all this idolatrous language current in the "conservative" press. "Homelands are born and die. They are complex, half spiritual and half physical, and in their foundation they carry a dirty burden of sin."

All these weaknesses help in loving and serving the homeland, but they advise against deifying it. The modern conception of the nation actually harms the cause of original homelands. "We desire our country to be great," says the *Esprit* group, "but we shall refuse it should it come at the price of its fidelity to justice." The nation, such as nationalists understand it, is placed above truth, justice, and individual rights. "We love our country before all others: it is natural law." *But not against the others.*

But not against the others. . . . Here is a position fixed with clarity. To love the homeland does not require lying, or hating, or preparing for war, or elevating the nation to the category of a metaphysical Totality, or confusing nation and State.

To work for the homeland is to make us all worthy of the possibility that it may be loved.

Notes

The source texts I have used in my translation of J. V. Foix's work come from the following editions: *Diari 1918*, ed. Joan Ramon Veny-Mesquida (Barcelona: Institut d'Estudis Catalans, 2004); *Gertrudis*, ed. Jaume Vallcorba (Barcelona: Quaderns Crema, 1983); *KRTU*, ed. Jaume Vallcorba (Barcelona: Quaderns Crema, 1983); and *Sobre literatura i art*, ed. Manuel Carbonell, vol. 4 of *Obres completes* (Barcelona: Edicions 62, 1990). For the text of the essay "Pàtria" ("Homeland"), I have relied on the version that appears in *Els lloms transparents* (The transparent book spines [Barcelona: Edicions 62, 1969]) as well as on the version printed in *La Publicitat* on 9 June 1935.

* * *

I have learned a great deal about Foix's life, his writing, and the landscape of Catalan culture in the early twentieth century from the work of various commentators. I would single out as especially helpful Foix's memoir, *Catalans de 1918* (Barcelona: Edicions 62, 1965); Vinyet Panyella's "intellectual biography," *J. V. Foix: 1918 i la idea catalana* (Barcelona: Edicions 62, 1989); and two essays by Joaquim Molas, "Sobre els dietaris de J. V. Foix" and "*Gertrudis* o l'aventura d'un jove poeta," in Molas's *Obra crítica* (Barcelona: Edicions 62, 1995), vol. 1, 419–44, 457–86. The annotations in Veny-Mesquida's critical edition of the *Diari 1918* have proven to be invaluable.

These publications comprise the main sources for the information about Foix's life and work provided in the following notes as well as in the introduction. The notes, however, incorporate a broader range of material in order to identify cultural and historical references, to indicate the publication history of specific texts, and to document the Catalan sources for

English translations included in the introduction. The aim is to build a more detailed context in which the anglophone reader can interpret Foix's writing.

xiv The first occasion when Foix presented himself as an "investigador en poesia" ("investigator in poetry") seems to have been his essay ". . . en versos ben tallat i arrodonida estrofa" (. . . in verses well cut and a stanza rounded off), which appeared in a magazine he coedited, *Quaderns de Poesia* 6 (January 1936), 1–4. Here he describes his "investigations" as "formal" (3–4).

xvi I translate the Catalan text of Joan Maragall's poem "L'ametller" from his *Obres completes: Poesies I* (Barcelona: Gustau Gili, 1912), 247:

> A mig aire de la serra
> veig un ametller florit:
> Déu te guard, bandera blanca,
> dies ha que t'he dalit!
> Ets la pau que s'anuncia
> entre el sol, núvols i vents . . .
> No ets encare el mellor temps
> prò'n tens tota l'alegria.

Foix's comments on Maragall's poetry appeared in *Catalans de 1918*, 25:

> Allà on hi ha espontaneïtat, la santa espontaneïtat—i jo voldria veure els esborranys dels càndid partidiaris de l'espontaneïtat—, hi ha gep. L'espontaneïtat del verb a cada mas, a cada individu—que són els dialects preferits per En Maragall—solen ésser l'esgarip i la paraulota.

xvii The Catalan text of Eugeni d'Ors's article "Coets" (Rockets) ran on the front page of *La Veu de Catalunya* on 23 June 1910 over his pseudonym, "Xènius":

> Ve una càlida nit de juny. Un barceloní puja al terrat, enjega un coet, y se recorda del cometa.

Com que del pas del cometa, ja'n fàdíes, y tot risch es passat, el barceloní s'entreté en un poch de filosofía, en un poch d'imatgería, sobre'l cometa.

Pensa: El cometa es al coet, lo que'l tigre es al gat. Un coet es un cometa domesticat.

Mes, — ¡paradoxa! — mentres la gracia dels cometes en estat selvatge, — dels estels ab cúa, consisteix en que compareixen segons càlcul, la gracia dels cometes en estat domèstich, — es a dir, dels coets, — consisteix en ésser imprevistos.

Això va contra dels qui sospiten que la civilitat resulta quelcom de fixo de geomètrich.

Al revès: El selvatgisme es sempre una cosa més fixa, perque deixa molt lloch a lo fatal. La civilitat es una divina flor de contingencia.

Pujeu, pujeu a les altures, coets imprevistos, coets contingents, — normes! — llibertats!

Foix's comments on d'Ors's style appeared in *Catalans de 1918*, 23, where he refers to its "deixes preciosistes i decadentistes de fi de segle":

el seu estil, per la meu gust, té un deix pre-rafaelita, ruskinià i àdhuc wildià que no es perd malgrat la forta dèria classicitzant del glossador, tan lucid, intel·ligent, sagaç i penetrant.

xviii Foix's familiarity with T. S. Eliot's writing is discussed by Lluís Cabré and Silvia Coll-Vinent, "J. V. Foix, traductor of T. S. Eliot (1927)," *Els Marges* 113 (2017), 55–73.

xix Enric Bou discusses the importance of "the unique geographical features of [Dalí's] homeland, as captured in his paintings and writings," in "From Foix to Dalí: Versions of Catalan Surrealism between Barcelona and Paris," *Artl@s Bulletin* 6:2 (Summer 2017), 44–52.

xxi In the *Manifeste du surréalisme* (1924), Breton presented his explanation of surrealism as an encyclopedia entry. I translate the passage from his *Œuvres completes,* ed. Marguerite Bonnet (Paris: Gallimard, 1988), vol. 1, 328:

> Le surréalisme repose sur la croyance à la réalité supérieure de certaines formes d'associations négligées jusqu'à lui, à la toute-puissance du rêve, au jeu désintéressé de la pensée.

Foix's piece "Textos Pràctiques" appeared in *L'Amic de les Arts* 29 (31 October 1928), 224–26, where he observes (225):

> La imatge hipnagògica és, uns cops, la il·luminació d'un mot pronunciat interiorment o d'una figura interiorment evocada. Altres cops, i aquestes són les que interessen, són la irrupció brusca d'unes visions netes, perfectes, sense relació amb el curs actual del pensament ni amb cap espectacle anterior.

xxiii Nancy J. Vickers examines the gender representations in European poetic traditions in "Diana Described: Scattered Women and Scattered Rhyme," *Critical Inquiry* 8 (1981), 265–79.

Breton's poem "L'Union libre" was first published anonymously in 1931 as an eleven-page chapbook by an unidentified Parisian press. I translate from the text in his *Poèmes* (Paris: Gallimard, 1948), 65:

> Ma femme à la bouche de cocarde et de bouquet
>   d'étoiles de dernière grandeur
> Aux dents d'empreintes de souris blanche sur la terre
>   blanche
> A la langue d'ambre et de verre frottés
> Ma femme à la langue d'hostie poignardée
> A la langue de poupée qui ouvre et ferme les yeux
> A la langue de pierre incroyable

xxiv I quote Freud's essay "On the Universal Tendency to Debasement in the Sphere of Love" (1912) from *The Standard Edition of the Complete Psychological Works of Sigmund Freud,* ed. and trans.

James Strachey (London: Hogarth Press and the Institute of Psycho-analysis, 1957), vol. 11, 177–90.

xxv I discuss the following reviews: Guillem Díaz-Plaja, "Ritme i rime en la prosa de J. V. Foix," *La Publicitat*, 16 October 1932, 5; Tomàs Garcés, "Un precursor," *La Publcitat*, 3 April 1927, front page; Domènec Guansé, "Les lletres," *Revista de Catalunya*, 35 (May 1927), 529–30; Rossend Llates, "Els Llibres: J. V. Foix, *KRTU*," *Mirador*, 191 (29 September 1932), 6; Lluís Montanyà, "A propòsit de *Gertrudis* de J. V. Foix," *La Nova Revista*, 4 (April 1927), 367–68; Manuel de Montoliu, "Breviari crítíc: J. V. Foix, *KRTU*," *La Veu de Catalunya*, 14 September 1932, 5; Pere Quart [Joan Oliver], "Degotís: *Gertrudis* de J. V. Foix," *Diari de Sabadell*, 1 April 1927, front page; and Carles Soldevila, "Full de dietari: Foix, primer sobre-realista català," *La Publicitat*, 27 March 1927, front page.

xxxvi Soldevila's snide comment reads:

> Aquest somnabulisme literari exigeix encara una forta dosi d'intel·ligència; en el fons del fons, el poeta o el narrador sobre-realista no renuncia a desvetllar-se en determinats moments i a donar un tust ràpid i invisible . . . És a dir, que no renuncia a fer trampa.

xxxvii Montanyà's detailed appreciation reads (367):

> Somni + lirisme + subconscient + intuïció + relativitat + retòrica + introspecció + lògica subjectiva + influències i/o coincidències: Reverdy-Einstein, Max-Jacob-Freud = Avantguardisme? Romanticisme? Classicisme? = Un avantguardista neo-romàntic classicitzant = J. V. FOIX.

Díaz-Plaja's explanation reads:

> En la puresa de tota subconsciència trobareu vetes de consciència, de raó, de memória. El mot dringa ordenadament i el poeta en pren la música o la suggestió. La resta és *creació derivada*.

xxviii Peter Cocozzella, review of J. V. Foix, *Diari 1918*, *World Literature Today* 57:1 (1983), 88.

xxix Harold Bloom, *The Western Canon: The Books and School of the Ages* (New York: Harcourt Brace, 1994), 548, 550.

David H. Rosenthal, ed. and trans., *When I Sleep, Then I See Clearly: Selected Poems of J. V. Foix* (New York: Persea, 1988).

xxx Jana Harris, "Outspoken Nationalist," *American Book Review* 12:4 (September/October 1990), 28.

xxxi I describe the development of my translation project, as well as the cultural issues it raises, in "Translation, Publishing, and World Literature: J. V. Foix's *Daybook 1918* and the Strangeness of Minority," *Translation Review* 92:3 (2016), 8–24.

xxxii Stephen [Stephanie] Burt, "The Elliptical Poets," in *Close Calls with Nonsense: Reading New Poetry* (Minneapolis, Minn.: Graywolf, 2009), 345–55.

2 The poet and critic Joaquim Folguera (1893–1919) admired such French avant-garde writers as Guillaume Apollinaire (1880–1918), Max Jacob (1876–1944), and Pierre Reverdy (1889–1960), whose work he translated into Catalan.

9 "Christ's last seven words" are expressions said to be spoken by Jesus Christ during his crucifixion and recorded in the gospels.

15 *"Papier d'Arménie"* (Armenian paper) is blotting paper infused with fragrant tincture of benzoin. It was invented in the late nineteenth century by a Frenchman who observed Armenians burning the shrub styrax to perfume and disinfect their homes.

The catalogue of women's names, "Ophelia, Virginie, Laura, Juliet," glances at famous literary heroines. The sources, in order, are Shakespeare's *Hamlet*, Jacques-Henri Bernardin de Saint-Pierre's novel *Paul et Virginie*, Petrarch's *Rime Sparse*, and Shakespeare's *Romeo and Juliet*.

19 "La Ribera" (The shore) locates the setting of this text in Sitges, a seaside town south of Barcelona. Trees were planted on the seafront there in the 1880s and 1890s, although they included palms.

20 The Catalan poet, critic, and translator Carles Riba (1893–1959) wrote poems in closed stanzaic structures with a tendency toward allegory. Among his translations into Catalan are Virgil's *Eclogues* (1911) and Homer's *Odyssey* (1919).

21 The term *gegant* refers to human figures made of papier-mâché, three to four meters high, which are paraded through Catalonian towns during festivals. Emerging in the fifteenth century, this folkloric tradition has extended into the present.

The Seu de Manresa is a Romanesque-Gothic basilica constructed from the eleventh to the sixteenth centuries in Manresa, a town in central Catalonia.

24 The painter Joan Miró (1893–1983) frequently collaborated with Foix, illustrating several of his works. He contributed the drawings for *Gertrudis* and *KRTU* that appear on pages xxxiv–xxxv.

27 The Spanish term *Via Crucis* refers to the Stations of the Cross, images that depict moments in Christ's crucifixion and form the basis of devotions in the Roman Catholic Church.

31 Spanish-language *La Vanguardia*, started in 1881, became one of Spain's leading daily newspapers, although it was based in Barcelona and engaged in Catalan cultural and political debates. *El Mundo Ilustrado*, started in 1879 and also based in Barcelona, billed itself as a "family library" focusing on "history, travel, science, art, and literature." It appealed to a middle-class readership with profuse illustrations and Spanish versions of articles by contemporary European authors.

Sant Pere Màrtir is a mountain (three hundred ninety meters) near Esplugues de Llobregat, a municipality within the Barcelona metropolitan area located southwest of the city.

33 By the late nineteenth century, as Albert Gonzàlez Masip documents in *Els tramvies de Barcelona: Història i explotació* (Barcelona: Rafael Dalmau, 1997), Barcelona was crossed by an extensive network of trams, initially horse-drawn, then steam-driven, and finally powered by electricity. The Plaça Catalunya, a large square in the center of the city, constituted a hub in the network. Pedralbes was a neighborhood in Sarrià, a predominantly rural village that became a district of Barcelona in 1921. Located northwest of the city, it was the area where Foix was born and lived throughout his life. The tramline Plaça Catalunya–Pedralbes transported Foix between Sarrià and Barcelona.

Gràcia was an independent village that became a district of Barcelona in 1897. Located in a northern area of the city, it was associated with radical political thinking, including Catalan nationalism and republicanism.

35 Ramon Rucabado (1884–1966) was a Catholic journalist who defended a staunchly Christian approach to moral and social issues. The French Symbolist poet, novelist, and critic Remy de Gourmont (1858–1915) formulated aesthetic and sexual theories that were strongly anticonformist. The poet and editor Josep Maria López-Picó (1886–1959) was influenced by the French Symbolists, although he invested their pursuit of pure poetry with religious significance. In 1915 he and Joaquim Folguera founded the Catalan cultural journal *La Revista*, to which many leading writers and intellectuals contributed, including Foix and Rucabado. It began as a monthly but soon shifted to biweekly publication, running until 1936.

37 Sant Vicenç, a square, and Clos de Sant Francesc, a street, are both located in Sarrià. La Violeta, which opened in 1886 in the same district, was a cultural center that offered classes in solfeggio for a working-class choir. It was also a popular dance hall.

Santa Eulàlia (c. 290–303 C.E.) suffered martyrdom for her Christian faith in Barcelona under the Roman emperor Diocletian. She became a patron saint of the city.

39 The French artist Gustave Doré (1832–1883) worked primarily with wood engravings, illustrating the works of such authors as Dante, John Milton, Lord Byron, and Edgar Allan Poe.

49 The name "Oscher" refers to the Scandinavian chieftain Asgeir (also spelled "Oscheri" and "Hoseri" in medieval chronicles). He was reported to have raided France in the ninth century, sacking such cities as Rouen and Bourdeaux.

53 The three texts titled "Notes del *Diari*" ("Notes from the *Daybook*") appeared in 1929 in the monthly magazine *Hèlix*, which promoted surrealism in Catalonia, publishing the work of André Breton (1896–1966), Luis Buñuel (1900–1983), and Joan Miró. It lasted for ten issues.

Trained as a lawyer, Alexandre Plana (1889–1940) later distinguished himself as a poet, fiction writer, and art critic. His poetics were *Noucentista*. His collection *El miralla imaginary* (The imaginary mirror, 1925) was among the first books of prose poetry in Catalan. He contributed some three hundred fifty articles to Catalan and Spanish periodicals, reviewing art exhibitions, films, plays, and phonograph recordings.

The reference to the initials A. B. can support various interpretations, none of which can be corroborated. Since the initials appear on earrings, for instance, they might refer to "aurora borealis," a term used to describe the lustrous appearance of jewelry gemstones like labradorite. Or the initials might refer to the Ateneu Barcelonès, where Plana frequently participated in literary discussion groups.

75 Can Pomeret was Foix's ancestral home in Sarrià.

97 Can Canet was a medieval farmhouse in Sarrià near the Reial Club de Tennis, which acquired the building in 1954.

99   Of the texts in this section, "Gertrudis" and "Christmas Story" were included in *Gertrudis*; the rest were published in *KRTU*.

101   The term "dragonite" refers to a fabulous stone which, according to Pliny's *Natural History* (37.57), derived from the brain of a dragon.

104   Carlism, a Spanish political movement that developed during the nineteenth century, aimed to establish a line of the Bourbon family on the Spanish throne.

105   Molins de Rei is a municipality located just west of Barcelona.

Built in the nineteenth century, the Diagonal is an avenue that bisects Barcelona from west to east. It is approximately eleven kilometers long and fifty meters wide throughout its length.

The *Pelayo* was a battleship active in the Spanish fleet between 1888 and 1925.

106   The Palazzo Giusti in Verona is a sixteenth-century building noted for its elaborately landscaped gardens. The Villa Giustiniani near Padua, the country seat of a Venetian family, was built from the fifteenth to the eighteenth centuries. It includes over five hectares of gardens. The Temple of Karnak is a huge complex of religious buildings constructed in the northern Egyptian city of Thebes over two millennia, beginning in the twenty-first century B.C.E.

107   Gold Flake was a brand of cigarettes introduced in 1878 and made by the British tobacco importer and cigarette manufacturer W. D. and H. O. Wills.

108   Josep Francesc Ràfols (1889–1965) was an art historian, painter, and architect who collaborated on the Sagrada Família, the cathedral built by Antoni Gaudí (1852–1926) in Barcelona. Among his publications was a study of the Italian Renaissance architect and engineer Filippo Brunelleschi. The architect Antoni Fisas (1896–1953) designed many Barcelona apartment buildings in the style of

Italianized classicism favored by *Noucentisme*. The Catalan poet Sebastià Sánchez-Juan (1904–1974) was influenced by Futurism.

French novelist and essayist Léon Bloy (1846–1917), after converting to Roman Catholicism, cultivated a powerfully polemical style through which he represented intense suffering as a means of redemption. The innovative plays, novels, and short stories of Luigi Pirandello (1867–1936) gained him an international reputation by the 1920s, culminating in the Nobel Prize for Literature in 1934. Pythagoras of Samos (c. 570–495 B.C.E.) was known as a philosopher and a mathematician, a cosmologist and a religious thinker who advocated a strict way of life.

La Publicitat, a Catalan daily newspaper published between 1922 and 1939, was acquired by the Catalanist political party Acció Catalana. Among its contributors were leading cultural figures of the period, including the philologist Pompeu Fabra (1868–1948), the writers Josep Pla (1897–1981) and Carles Riba, and the politician Antoni Rovira i Virgili (1882–1949). Foix edited the literary section between 1923 and 1936.

110   The Catalan text for "Deserted paths, lifeless thoroughfares" opened *KRTU*:

> Pistes desertes, avingudes mortes,
> ombres sense ombra per cales i platges,
> pujols de cendra en els més folls viratges,
> trofeus d'amor per finestres i portes.
>
> A quin indret, oh ma follia, emportes
> aquest cos meu que no tem els oratges,
> ni el meravellen els mòbils paratges
> ni els mil espectres de viles somortes?
>
> No sé períbol en la terra obscura
> que ajusti el gest i la passa diversa
> a qui la solitud li és bell viure.

No hi ha caserna ni presó tan dura,
no hi ha galera en la mar més adversa
que em faci prou esclau i ésser més lliure?

Foix's epigraph is the first line of Petrarch's poem. Here is the text given in Robert Durling's *Petrarch's Lyric Poems: The "Rime Sparse" and Other Lyrics* (Cambridge, Mass.: Harvard University Press, 1976), 95:

Solo e pensoso i piú deserti campi
vo mesurando a passi tardi e lenti,
et gli occhi porto per fuggire intenti
ove vestigio uman la rena stampi.

Altro schermo non trovo che mi scampi
dal manifesto accorger de le genti,
perché negli atti d'allegrezza spenti
di fuor si legge com'io dentro avampi.

Sì ch'io mi credo omai che monti et piagge
et fiumi et selve sappian di che temper
sia la mia vita, ch'è celata altrui;

ma pur sì aspre vie né sì selvage
cercar non so, ch'Amor non venga sempre
ragionando con meco, ed io con lui.

Durling provides this English version (94):

Alone and filled with care, I go measuring the most deserted fields with steps delaying and slow, and I keep my eyes intent so as to flee from where any human footprint marks the sand.

No other shield do I find to protect me from people's open knowing, for in my bearing, in which all happiness is extinguished, anyone can read from without how I am aflame within.

So that I believe by now that mountains and slopes and rivers and woods know the temper of my life, which is hidden from other persons;

but still I cannot seek paths so harsh or so savage that Love does not always come along discoursing with me and I with him.

113 El Port de la Selva is a fishing village on the Costa Brava in the far northeastern corner of Catalonia. In 1930 its population was 1,050.

The Port de Reig is a harbor used as a marina in El Port de la Selva.

The Cova Colomera is a chasm in the foothills of the Pyrenees, located in the fluvial gorge known as the Congost de Mont Rebei.

114 The Cap de Creus is a peninsula in Catalonia approximately twenty-five kilometers from the French border. El Port de la Selva is situated on the northern coast of the Cap de Creus.

115 The name "Teiera" is apparently a local usage applied to a rock formation at El Port de la Selva, although it appears on no maps. The term suggests that the rock is shaped like the medieval lighting device known as a *teiera*, a circular iron grill in which resinous wood was burnt. The "rock Teiera" would thus contain openings through which the sunrise (it is "facing east") might be visible on the horizon.

116 Foix gave the title *Presentacions* to his verbal portraits of the three Catalan painters. I translate this title as *Introductions*.

In 1906 the art dealer Josep Dalmau (1867–1937) opened the Galeries Dalmau in Barcelona, and until 1930, when it closed, he promoted the work of European avant-garde artists. The subjects of his exhibitions included Cubist painters (1912), Kees van Dongen (1915), Joan Miró (1918), Francis Picabia (1922), and Salvador Dalí (1925).

Foix's "introduction" of Dalí (1904–1989) sketches a veritable map of central Barcelona. By the beginning of the twentieth century, the boulevard known as the Passeig de Gràcia had become the city's most elegant street, the site of luxury hotels and innovative buildings designed by such *Modernista* architects as Gaudí and Lluís Domènech (1850–1923). The Carrer de la Diputació is a street that intersects the Passeig de Gràcia a few blocks above the Plaça Catalunya. The Carrer de Provença and Carrer d'Aragó are located just beyond Diputació.

Founded by a group of horseback riding enthusiasts, the Cercle Eqüestre subsequently became a private club that drew its members from the Barcelona elite. In 1926 it was housed in an opulent building on the Passeig de Gràcia.

117 In 1927 Dalí painted two Cubist-inspired works, titled *Harlequin* and *Mannequin*.

119 Sant Gervasi is a northwestern district of Barcelona that borders on Sarrià.

In 1918 the Galeries Dalmau was located on the Carrer de la Portaferrissa in the Barri Gòtic, the medieval quarter of Barcelona.

120 The art critic M. A. Cassanyes (1893–1956) wrote about the avantgarde movements for such Catalan periodicals as *L'Amic de les Arts* and *La Publicitat*. He occasionally curated exhibitions, including a 1929 group show at the Galeries Dalmau which included artists like Hans Arp and Piet Mondrian.

Between 1924 and 1929, while a new underground station was being constructed for the train to Sarrià, a temporary terminus was located on the Ronda de la Universitat, a boulevard that runs from the Universitat de Barcelona to Plaça Catalunya.

121 Born in Sitges, Artur Carbonell (1906–1973) was a surrealist painter who also directed theatrical productions, including Catalan translations of the work of such playwrights as Jean Cocteau, Eugene O'Neill, Luigi Pirandello, Arthur Schnitzler, George Bernard Shaw,

and August Strindberg. In 1930 Foix was involved in organizing a one-man show of Carbonell's paintings at the Galería Areñas in Barcelona.

The Sant Sebastià beach in Sitges is roughly two hundred meters long and twenty meters wide. It is located a short distance from the parish church, Sant Bartomeu.

122 Foix added a footnote to this text when it was published in *KRTU*: "The initial paragraph of the lecture, 'Texts and Applications,' delivered at 'El Centaure' in Sitges, September 1928, to accompany texts relating to Poe, Valéry, Blake, and Lautréamont as well as an exhibition concerning what is understood by hypnagogic images." Foix, however, gave an incorrect date: the event took place on 13 May 1928. He was joined by the editorial staff of the magazine *L'Amic de les Arts*, where he published his lecture on 31 October of the same year. The other speakers included M. A. Cassanyes, Salvador Dalí, and Sebastià Sánchez-Juan.

123 "Poldo" is a shortened form of the name "Leopoldo."

Solsona is a town in the province of Lleida, located roughly in the center of Catalonia. It has a tradition of *gegants* that dates back to the seventeenth century.

The *Noucentista* sculptor Ernest Maragall (1903–1991), son of the Catalan poet Joan Maragall, began exhibiting his work in the 1920s.

The Latin phrase, meaning "Glory to God in the Highest," is the beginning of the Christian hymn known as the "Greater Doxology." It celebrates the birth of Christ.

In 1928 Ford began producing its Model A car, and by 1931 it had sold over five million. Mathis, a French car manufacturer in Alsace that operated between 1910 and 1950, produced twenty thousand cars in 1927, ranking fourth after Citroën, Renault, and Peugeot. Mathis models were typically identified with one or two digits.

124 The Garraf, a limestone massif on the coast of Catalonia south of Barcelona, contains hundreds of caves and sinkholes.

129 "Avant-gardism" appeared under Foix's byline on the front page of the *Monitor: Gaseta Nacional de Política, d'Art i de Literatura,* 1:2 (February 1921). Edited by Foix and the Catalanist Josep Carbonell (1897–1979), the *Monitor* began as a monthly magazine but soon published irregularly. It ran for nine issues from 1921 to 1923.

Carles Soldevila (1892–1967) championed *Noucentista* values in prose fiction and drama designed to refine bourgeois culture in Barcelona.

130 Here and throughout I use "homeland" to translate Foix's references to the "pàtria," a Catalan word that can also be rendered as "fatherland" and "native country."

131 The parenthetical quotation presents a roll call of contemporary French poets, novelists, and dramatists which moves from idealists who cultivated traditional literary forms to iconoclasts who advocated modernist experimentalism: Romain Rolland (1866–1944), Paul Claudel (1868–1955), Guillaume Apollinaire, and Tristan Tzara (1896–1963).

135 "Some Considerations on Current Literature and Art" was published under Foix's byline in *L'Amic de les Arts,* 20 (30 November 1927), 104–6. Headed by Josep Carbonell, who oversaw a team of editors that included Foix, the monthly *L'Amic de les Arts* ran for thirty-one issues from 1926 to 1929.

137 A working-class autodidact based in Barcelona, Joan Salvat-Papasseit (1894–1924) wrote political prose in both Castilian and Catalan in which he adopted a range of ideological positions—Christian, socialist, anarchist, Catalanist. His Catalan lyric poetry shows the influence of Apollinaire's calligrams as well as the adulation of technology expressed by the Futurist Filippo Tommaso Marinetti (1876–1944).

139   The Catholic priest Norbert Font i Sagué (1874–1910) was a geol-
      ogist who introduced speleology into Catalonia through a number
      of popular works. In 1898 he explored two deep sinkholes in the
      Garraf—the Bruc (one hundred eighteen meters) and La Ferla (one
      hundred eighty-one meters). The lake he reported having seen in
      the Bruc has never been found.

140   The French writers Pierre de Ronsard (1524–1585) and Jean Racine
      (1639–1699) enjoyed fame akin to canonicity in their lifetimes.
      Within the eighty years following Dante's death in 1320, his *Divine
      Comedy* achieved canonical status through commentaries.

      The French naturalist Jean-Baptiste Lamarck (1744–1829) devel-
      oped a theory of evolution based on adaptation to the environment.

142   Born in Vic, the Catholic priest Jaume Balmes (1810–1848) addressed
      philosophical and political topics in Spanish-language works.

144   "Some Reflections on One's Own Literature" was published under
      Foix's byline in *L'Amic de les Arts*, 31 (31 March 1929), 11–12. A
      revised version was published as a preface to *KRTU*, where in a foot-
      note Foix stated that "this text, dated 12 February 1929, responds
      to a questionnaire developed by *L'Amic de les Arts*." This revised
      version was reprinted with the title "Proleg del Llibre 'KRTU' " in
      La Publicitat, 17 June 1932, 3. Further changes were introduced in
      the editions of Foix's collected works that began appearing with the
      Obres poètiques (Barcelona: Nauta, 1964), which he saw through
      the press. I have based my translation on the 1983 critical edition
      published by Quaderns Crema. In the notes that follow I will indi-
      cate textual variants with the italicized dates when they appeared:
      1929, 1932, and *1964.*

      Foix later identified the "illustrious critic" as Carles Riba in an inter-
      view; see Albert Manent, "Entre la llegenda i la vida de cada dia,"
      Serra d'Or 160 (January 1973), 20–26.

Trossos (Pieces) ran for six issues between 1916 and 1918. It was edited by the art critic and poet Josep Maria Junoy (1887–1955), who was also the author of the first calligram in Catalan.

The French magazine *Littérature* was edited by Breton, Philippe Soupault, and Louis Aragon between 1919 and 1924. Although the respondents to the survey were overwhelmingly French, they included two foreign writers: Giuseppe Ungaretti and Knut Hamsun. Foix provides only the responses; I have inserted the names of the respondents. He quotes from two issues of *Littérature*: 10 (December 1919), 24, 26, and 12 (February 1920), 26.

L'Amic de les Arts was the name of a press as well as a magazine. It published both *Gertrudis* and *KRTU*.

145 Both *1929* and *1932* describe "our exhibition" as "shameless" and "my psychic states" as "my psychic spasms." The word "states" is introduced in *1964*. The "someone who wrote with conviction" is called "stupid, imbecilic, idiotic" in *1929*.

The reference to the "thoughtful request" glances at the *L'Amic de les Arts* questionnaire that occasioned this essay.

1929 describes the "ambition" not as "youthful" but as "Napoleonic." In both *1929* and *1932* the phrase "prose poems I have written" is qualified by a parenthetical remark: "most of which I have transcribed." The remark is deleted from *1964*.

My use of "retreat" translates Foix's Catalan word "retrocés," which derives from "retrocedir" (in English "to turn back" or "to move backward"). Other possible translations of "retrocés" include "pullback," "withdrawal," "regression." I have italicized the word here and elsewhere in the essay; Foix put it within quotation marks. In the handwritten corrections that Foix made to his copy of *1964*, "retrocés" is emended to "repressió." The first Catalan translations of Freud's key terms appeared in the synthesis of psychoanalytic research published by Emili Mir in *Monografies mèdiques* (Barcelona: Llibreria Catalònia, 1926), where "Verdrängung" is rendered as "repressió."

The French word "refoulement" appears italicized in Foix's Catalan text. French translators of Freud's works used it to render "Verdrängung"; see, for instance, Sigmund Freud, *Introduction à la psychanalyse*, trans. Samuel Jankélévitch (Paris: Payot, 1921).

146   In both *1929* and *1932* the "liberation" that is "permitted" by the "second group" of prose poems occurs "under the suggestion of several literary schools." This phrase is deleted from *1964*.

Both *1929* and *1932* describe the "mysterious streets without end" not as those "where the weak get lost" but as those "which symbolize my utter ethical defeat." The revision occurs in *1964*.

I translate Foix's Catalan word "pràctiques" as "applications" and replace his quotation marks with italics.

In *1929* the "frail and frivolous" texts are said to "have pleased a remarkable group of fanatics."

In referring to "Pepa the Milkmaid" as "frail and frivolous," Foix is taking a swipe at the Catalan poet and playwright Joan Oliver (1889–1986), who under the pseudonym Pere Quart reviewed *Gertrudis* for the *Diari de Sabadell*. Oliver singled out that prose poem, praising it as "a transparent and fresh liquid that leaves an ineffable taste" ("liquid transparent i fresc que deixa un sabor ineffable").

Both *1929* and *1932* describe "the position of our literature" not as "loyal" but as "the most logical." The revision occurs in *1964*.

147   "Homeland," titled "Pàtria" in Catalan, was published under Foix's pseudonym, "Focius," in *La Publicitat*, 9 June 1935, 9. It was later revised at points and included in his collection of newspaper columns, *Els lloms transparents*, 130–33. I have based my translation primarily on the 1969 edition, but I have incorporated variants from the 1935 version. In notes that follow I will indicate these variants with the italicized dates when they appeared: *1935* and *1969*.

The word "absolute" appears only in *1935*.

Charles Maurras (1868–1952) was the main ideologist of Action Française, a reactionary political movement that promulgated nationalism, monarchism, and anti-Semitism. Kliment Voroshilov (1881–1969), a Soviet military officer, carried out Stalinist purges during the 1930s. Playwright and novelist Romain Rolland won the Nobel Prize for Literature in 1915. In the wake of World War I, hoping to promote world peace, Rolland imagined an international community of intellectuals who were independent of political institutions and movements.

In 1969 the word "individual" is deleted and the phrase "local or tribal" added.

Only in 1935 does the word "patriot" appear after "oppressed," and the word "bloody" before "annihilation."

The Empordà is the northeastern region of Catalonia which borders on France.

In 1969 the word "Andalusian" is deleted.

148 Founded in 1932, the French journal *Esprit* established itself as the organ of "personalism," an individualistic philosophy that advocates intellectual independence and transcendental values. In the 1930s it opposed not only materialisms, whether capitalist or communist, but also the values advanced by fascism. Foix cites the "manifesto" titled "Notre Patrie: Déclaration collective," which appeared in *Esprit* 3:30 (1 June 1935), 339–48. His earlier reference to the "interest," the "reason," and the "truth" of the "State" is a partial translation from the French text, but neither 1935 nor 1969 puts the translated phrases within quotation marks.

149 Louis-Jean Malvy (1875–1949), a member of the center-left Radical Party in France, was a representative in the Chamber of Deputies (1906–1919, 1924–1942). He also served in ministerial positions: Commerce, Industry, Posts and Telegraphs (1913–1914) and Interior (1914–1917, March–June 1926). In 1918 a charge of treason led to his exile for five years. Jean Chiappe (1878–1940), a French civil servant whose politics were conservative, was appointed director of

General Security in the 1920s and prefect of police in the 1930s. Chiappe banned Luis Buñuel and Salvador Dalí's film, *L'Age d'or* (1930).

1969 refers only to "absolute States." The account of "totalitarian States" that ends the paragraph appears in *1935*. There it is put within quotation marks, indicating that Foix is presenting his Catalan translation from the *Esprit* manifesto. In *1935* the quotation begins at the phrase "the more human and universal." The quotation marks are deleted in *1969*.

In *1969* "conservative" replaces "rightist" in describing the "press."

In the sentence that begins with "the nation, such as nationalists understand it," as well as the phrase "against the others," Foix translates portions of the *Esprit* manifesto. Neither *1935* nor *1969* puts the translated material within quotation marks.

150 The dense logic of Foix's final sentence departs from the more straightforward syntax that concludes the French text in *Esprit*: "work with us to reconstruct a France worthy of being loved" ("travaillez avec nous à reconstruire une France digne d'être aimée"). Foix's Catalan text reads: "Treballar per la Pàtria és fer-nos tots dignes que sigui estimada." I have inserted the word "possibility" to underscore the subjunctive mood of "sigui estimada" as well as to make the syntax more fluent.

CPSIA information can be obtained
at www.ICGtesting.com
Printed in the USA
FSHW021401030220
66772FS